ANAÏS NIN'S LOST WORLD

By Britt Arenander

Britt Arenander

Anaïs Nin's Lost World

Paris in Words and Pictures, 1924-1939

SKY BLUE PRESS

COPYRIGHT INFORMATION

Text copyright © 2017 Britt Arenander

Photos copyright © photographers/rights holders listed below

Book layout copyright © 2017 Sky Blue Press

All rights reserved. No part of this book may be reproduced in any form or by electronic or mechanical means, including information storage and retrieval systems, without permission in writing from the publisher, except by a reviewer who may quote brief passages in a review.

SKY BLUE PRESS
Gaithersburg, Maryland

Library of Congress Cataloging-in-Publication Data

Names: Arenander, Britt, 1941-
Title: Anais Nin's lost world : Paris in words and pictures, 1924-1939 / By Britt Arenander.
Other titles: Anais Nins förlorade värld. English
Description: First American paperback edition. | Gaithersburg, MD : Sky Blue Press, [2017] | Includes bibliographical references.
Identifiers: LCCN 2017034318 | ISBN 9780998724645 (pbk.)
Subjects: LCSH: Nin, Anaïs, 1903-1977--Homes and haunts--France--Paris. | Nin, Anaïs, 1903-1977--Friends and associates. | Paris (France)--Social life and customs--20th century. | Americans--France--Paris--History--20th century.
Classification: LCC PS3527.I865 Z54713 2017 | DDC 818/.5209 [B] --dc23
LC record available at https://lccn.loc.gov/2017034318

TABLE OF CONTENTS

Cover photo: Hugh Guiler at rue Schoelcher, below one of the windows of his and Anaïs's apartment, looking up at Anaïs.

Introduction 9

Before Louveciennes (1924-1930) 11
    Fig. 1: Rue d'Assas ....
    Fig. 2: Hôtel Orfila 14-15
    Fig. 3: Café Zeyer 18
    Fig. 4: Le Dôme 19
    Fig. 5: The Jockey 19
    Fig. 6: Avenue Foch 20-21
    Fig. 7: Rue Schoelcher 23
    Fig. 8: Nin apartment, 11 bis rue Schoelcher 24
    Fig. 9: 47 boulevard Suchet 29
    Fig. 10: Interior 47 boulevard Suchet 28
    Fig. 11: Chemin de fer de ceinture 29

Louveciennes (1930-1936) 31
    Fig. 12: Gare St-Lazare 33
    Fig. 13: Louveciennes train station, ca. 1930 34
    Fig. 14: 2 bis rue de Montbuisson, ca. 1900 35
    Fig. 15: M. Leboeuf at Louveciennes, ca. 1900 36
    Fig. 16: 2 bis rue de Montbuisson, 1931 37
    Fig. 17: 2 bis rue de Montbuisson, mid-1990s 38
    Fig. 18: 2 bis rue de Montbuisson, mid-1990s 38
    Fig. 19: Mme. Leboeuf at Louveciennes, ca. 1900 39
    Fig. 20: Back of 2 bis rue de Montbuisson, mid-1990s 40-41
    Fig. 21: Château de Louveciennes 43
    Fig. 22: 4 rue Delambre 44
    Fig. 23: Place de l'Odéon 45
    Fig. 24: Henry Miller, ca. 1932 46
    Fig. 25: Hôtel Central 48
    Fig. 26: View from Hôtel Central 49
    Fig. 27: Rue Scribe 50-51
    Fig. 28: Anaïs Nin at Louveciennes, ca. 1932 55

Fig. 29: 5 rue Lamartine 56

Fig. 30: Hôtel Cronstadt 57

Fig. 31: Place de Clichy 59

Fig. 32: Avenue Anatole France, Clichy 60-61

Fig. 33: Rue de Neuilly, Clichy 62

Fig. 34: Miller residence, Clichy 63

Fig. 35: Brothel, 32 rue Blondel 64

Fig. 36: Porte St-Martin 65

Fig. 37: René Allendy residence 67

Fig. 38: Zadkine museum 69

Fig. 39: Otto Rank residence 71

Fig. 40: Hotel, 26, rue des Marronniers 72

Fig. 41: 18 Villa Seurat 74

Fig. 42: Villa Seurat 75

After Louveciennes (1936-1939) 79

Fig. 43: Nin apartment, 30 quai de Passy 81

Fig. 44: Quai de Passy 82-83

Fig. 45: Quai des Tuileries 85

Fig. 46: View of the Seine from quai de Passy 86-87

Fig. 47: La Coupole 89

Fig. 48: La Belle Aurore 90

Fig. 49: Nin apartment, 12 rue Cassini 92

Fig. 50: Anaïs Nin's birthplace, Neuilly 93

Fig. 51: Preparation for war, 1939 95

Fig. 52: Artistic preparation for war, 1939 95

References 97

Author's Note 98

About the Author 98

Photo Credits 99

Index 100

INTRODUCTION

When, some years ago, I was lucky enough to move to France the idea came to me that I would finally look up the mythical house in Louveciennes where Anaïs Nin lived when she met Henry Miller for the first time. Furthermore I was just then translating the unexpurgated diary, *Henry and June*, and was once more thrust back into Anaïs Nin's enchanted Paris.

In Louveciennes I did what many Anaïs Nin admirers probably did then: I took snapshots of the sadly uninhabited house through the rusty iron gate, and then decided to climb over hedges and walls to enter the premises behind the house, the "wild garden," where I also took photos.

The next day I continued my pilgrimage to 4, avenue Anatole France in Clichy and found, amazingly, that the building where Henry Miller and Alfred Perlès rented their modest flat in 1932 was still there. Why not check if the house at 18, Villa Seurat perhaps remained, too, as in Miller's and Nin's time? It did.

The more places I sought out, the more delighted I was to discover that most of Nin's and Miller's former homes and hangouts were still there, spared from mad city planners. Slowly the idea was born of reconstructing some of the Paris that Nin and Miller had lived in and loved. My own photos from Louveciennes were just a start; now I had to find old postcards, photos from museum archives, from private photo albums.

Assisted by the town hall of Louveciennes, I got in touch with the then owner of the house at 2, rue de Montbuisson, Monsieur Pierre Auzépy, a retired physician living in Paris. He let me use photos of the house at Louveciennes from his old family album. I also searched through museum archives, the weekly postcard market held in the outskirts of Paris, and the small shops specializing in old postcards. I sought out every address at which Anaïs and Henry had lived, every house, hotel, bar and restaurant, every street and block specifically mentioned by them in novels, diaries and letters.

Thus I discovered that the Hôtel Central in Montparnasse, where their passionate liaison was initiated in a shabby little room on the fifth floor, is still there, as well as the building where the legendary *Chicago Tribune* was housed; Henry Miller's favorite hotel opposite the *Tribune*, Hôtel Cronstadt; René Allendy's three-story house on rue de l'Assomption; no. 9, rue Louis Boilly where Otto Rank lived and worked; and 60, rue d'Assas, where Anaïs and her husband Hugh Guiler lodged in a boarding house when they arrived in Paris in December 1924, a place that turned out to be August Strindberg's famous Hôtel Orfila...

The peak of my research occurred quite unexpectedly in a small shop in the 13th arrondissement, where all of a sudden I found myself staring at a postcard of avenue Anatole France in Clichy, from 1932! I hadn't even dreamt that someone would have considered it worth immortalizing this street, but then I discovered that in the early '30s the apartment houses being built on avenue Anatole France were the pride of Clichy: decent and attractive-looking housing for the working people, where Miller and his friend Alfred Perlès lived.

A lost world, of which the outlines still remain, was what I wished to recreate, by help of photographic jigsaw puzzle pieces. But my hope is also that it might be an intimate guide to Paris outside the main tourist routes.

Britt Arenander

Anaïs Nin, Paris, 1929

BEFORE LOUVECIENNES

(1924 – 1930)

Anaïs Nin in Richmond Hill, New York just before the move to France.

For many of Anaïs Nin's readers, her life in Paris is above all linked to Louveciennes and her liaison with Henry Miller at the beginning of the '30s. But Anaïs had already lived for six years in Paris with her husband Hugh Guiler when they, for financial reasons due to the great crash, found themselves forced to move from Paris to Louveciennes in September 1930.

Anaïs and Hugh got married in Cuba in March 1923, when Anaïs was 20 and Hugh 25; upon returning to the U.S. they installed themselves in Queens, New York, where Anaïs's mother, Rosa Culmell-Nin, also lived with her sons Thorvald and Joaquín. Mrs. Culmell-Nin was the owner of a brownstone house where she let rooms, but she was struggling with overwhelming economic problems and had to sell the property. Thus she decided to go to Paris with Thorvald and Joaquín, principally to let Joaquín study music there. Hugh Guiler, who was employed at the First National Bank (which later changed its name to City Bank) in New York, suggested that he ask to be transferred to the bank's Parisian branch office, partly because he knew that Anaïs was very much attached to her family, and partly because he himself would be delighted to spend time in Paris.

In June 1924 Anaïs writes in her diary that Hugh had started to make demands about a transfer to Paris. Anaïs herself was quite excited at the prospect of moving "to the Paris of Balzac, Flaubert and Anatole France, to the Paris of the poets, of Dumas and Victor Hugo" (*Early Diary 3*, p. 43). Paris was actually her birthplace (she was born in the suburb of Neuilly in 1903) but, as she had no memory of that early period, she didn't feel that she was returning home so much as launching herself on a new adventure.

In July 1924 the Guilers were told that Hugh's application for a post at the First National Bank's branch office in Paris had been granted and that he was to start his new job in January 1925. Rosa Culmell-Nin had already left the U.S. with Thorvald and Joaquín in August 1924, and judging from the letters that Anaïs received from her it seems that they had adapted well to Paris.

Following page:
Fig. 1. Rue d'Assas at the intersection of rue du Cherche Midi; the photograph was probably taken around the turn of the twentieth century. The boarding house where Anaïs and Hugh lodged in 1925 is situated farther down the street, on the right.

Previous page:
Fig. 2. The boarding house at 60, rue d'Assas was earlier called Hôtel Orfila. Today there is a memorial plate beside the entrance saying that August Strindberg lived there from February to July 1896. The house, built in 1825, has been somewhat modified, and more floors have been added to the small, low house on the left. It's in that house that we find the entrance door nos. 60-62 today. The original entrance door to no. 60 in the bigger building has been closed. In 1925, however, the building looked exactly as it had at the time of Strindberg.

Anaïs and Hugh didn't leave New York until December 17, 1924. On the ship they made the acquaintance of Horace Guiccardi, a gallant French count whom they were to see quite a lot in Paris and who appeared as the incarnation of Parisian depravity to the young and puritanical Anaïs.

Anaïs's first diary note after her arrival in Paris, dated December 1924, gives evidence of a culture shock: compared to New York, Paris was grey, dull and revoltingly dirty, and the Parisians in their worn clothes made a disheartening impression. But when Anaïs complained about this, Hugh mildly corrected her: Paris was not dirty, just old.

During this first period the Guilers lived in an anonymous hotel not far from the rue du Bac, in the 7th arrondissement on the left bank, where most of the guests were American. After only a few days in Paris, Anaïs went to visit her father, the Spanish concert pianist Joaquín Nin Sr., who had abandoned his family in 1913 when Anaïs was ten years old. He now lived on an elegant block of Paris with his mistress, Maruca, whom Anaïs had met just before her father left his family and whom he was now about to marry. Anaïs immediately felt sympathetic towards "la petite dame" and found that she had been a good influence on her father, about whom she writes very critically in her diary; she felt that he was sentimental and unreliable, and she simply couldn't respond to his demonstrativeness. Her brothers didn't want to meet their father at all, and Anaïs refused to give him their address.

On January 3, 1925, the Guilers moved to a pension, or boarding house, at 60, rue d'Assas in Montparnasse. Anaïs seemed unaware that she and Hugh had ended up in Strindberg's old Hôtel Orfila, as she didn't mention anything about it in her diary.

Before World War I, Montparnasse had already started to replace Montmartre as the main attraction for all the artists and bohemians streaming to Paris, and a cosmopolitan colony had developed in now-legendary cafés such as Le Dôme, La Rotonde and La Closerie des Lilas, in those days very simple, inexpensive places.

In her memoirs, the Swedish artist Thora Dardel describes her own disappointment at La Rotonde: "A filthy, stinking, rowdy hole with sawdust on the floor and the scariest blokes at every table." But she soon learned to appreciate the shabby, smoky, cosmopolitan atmosphere of La Rotonde, where pioneers like Modigliani, Rodin and Brancusi were daily guests.

When a new generation of international artists began filling the cafés of Montparnasse after the horrible break between 1914-18, the Americans were soon to dominate the scene. Fleeing the prohibition and the puritanism of their native country, they came to have the time of their lives during "les années folles." At the brasseries American-style bars were installed, and by the mid-'20s, when Anaïs and Hugh arrived in Paris, the nocturnal life at Le Dôme, Le Select and La Rotonde was in full swing.

As a matter of fact, Montparnasse was not a particularly attractive district. The Hungarian photographer Georges Brassaï (alias Gyula Halász), later to be famous for his documentation of Paris of the '30s and for his portraits of the future celebrities then flocking there, described Montparnasse as completely devoid of charm, "un-picturesque" and without character, and he found its magnetism inexplicable.

Anaïs and Hugh, however, had arrived close to the boulevard de Montparnasse accidentally, but launching themselves into a bohemian way of life was for the moment out of question. Anaïs was totally intent on being a good wife helping her husband in his career, and moreover her family was in need of her assistance: to her alarm she found them living in a cold and uncomfortable attic flat, where, on top of everything else, Joaquín Jr. had contracted tuberculosis.

Fig. 3. Avenue du Maine runs through Montparnasse from Gare Montparnasse to Place Victor Basch, metro Alésia, where one of Anaïs's and Henry's favorite places, Café Zeyer, was situated, at 62, rue d'Alésia. It's still there, but devoid of its former atmosphere.

When Anaïs wasn't busy mending socks and sewing buttons on for Hugh or helping Rosa and her brothers, she worked on a novel and a play or went for long, lonely walks in the city that from the beginning aroused her aversion. Not only was it dirty and old-fashioned, worn and uncomfortable, the climate was dreadful. It was cold, it rained a lot, the streets were wet and muddy and the perpetual honking of the cars got on her nerves. "Paris was gloomy," she writes in her diary, "mother downhearted. The pension impossible" (*Early Diary 3*, p. 84).

She complains about the humid sheets, the naked bulb hanging from the ceiling, the moldy wallpaper making her sick, and she regrets that they ever left New York.

Fig. 4. Le Dôme in the '20s, one of the four mythical hangouts of the cosmopolitan colony in Montparnasse. Located at 108, boulevard du Montparnasse.

Fig. 5. The Jockey, the oldest cabaret in Montparnasse, decorated by American painter Hilaire Hiler, whom Anaïs got to know in the mid-'30s. He played the piano there in the evenings, sometimes to accompany the legendary singer Kiki.

Previous page:
Fig. 6. Avenue Foch, one of the avenues starting from L'Arc de Triomphe, opposite avenue Hoche, where Anaïs and Hugh stayed in a small flat at no. 15 for a couple of months in 1925, before they found an apartment of their own.

Occasionally she made an effort to look on the bright side, as when she argues with herself in the diary about great artists and writers who had lived in rooms far more miserable than hers: "They have gone out under the rain and returned to musty and damp rooms and seen such furniture as we have seen, and even similar wallpaper, without losing their cheerfulness and their wits," she writes in January 1925 (p. 85).

Only a couple days after her upbeat diary entry, Anaïs admits that she is not strong enough to bear the cold, the rain and the dirt.

Her brother Thorvald soon had enough of Paris. On January 9, 1925, he left for Havana, where he was going to live with his aunt. Thorvald, who later became a businessman, was to remain in Latin America for most of his life. Rosa and Joaquín also left the unhealthy Paris for a while, so that Joaquín could breathe fresh air by the sea.

At the end of January 1925, Anaïs and Hugh were offered the opportunity to live for a couple of months in a private apartment and were happy to leave "the flowery paper, the daily cabbage and beans and potatoes, the mustiness, the peculiar boarding house atmosphere of the pension..." (*Early Diary 3*, p. 98). They moved to 15, avenue Hoche, one of the avenues spreading out from L'Arc de Triomphe, where they borrowed an apartment belonging to a certain Mr. Hansen, a colleague of Hugh's who was going away for a period. It consisted of two rooms and a kitchen overlooking a dark back yard, but after the boarding house the flat was almost a home. Anaïs writes in her diary that after she had "taken down 52 pictures of horses and nude women," she rearranged the furniture and unpacked their books and ornaments, including their "familiar blue pottery" and copper candlesticks (p. 98).

When Mr. Hansen returned in the spring of 1925, Anaïs and Hugh moved to another boarding house, this time at 22, rue Pauquet (now rue Jean Giraudoux in the fashionable 16th arrondissement), where they lodged at the beginning of April. The place was more pleasant than the gloomy boarding house at rue d'Assas, with a big, well-lit room overlooking the street. Anaïs admits that she is happy not having to cook anymore.

But in spite of now living in a comfortable place and seeing spring turn into summer—one that F. Scott Fitzgerald would later call "the summer of the thousand parties"—Anaïs failed to discover the charm of Paris. In July 1925 she writes in her diary: "Oh, I wish we were out of Paris, and there are moments the two years which we must spend here seem interminable and terrible to me" (*Early Diary 3*, pp. 151-152).

At the end of August 1925, the Guilers finally found a flat of their own, at 11 bis, rue Schoelcher, not far from Place Denfert-Rochereau, close to the Montparnasse cemetery. Together with Horace Guiccardi's wife, Anaïs had gone to see a flat to rent at rue Schoelcher but found it dull and unattractive.

Out on the street again, her eyes fell on a "new, white building" on the same street, with big bay windows hinting that there might be artists' studios within (p. 152). Anaïs immediately found out that there were several studios to let, and four days later Hugh signed the contract for the apartment where they were to live for four years. They were also able to rent an apartment for Rosa and Joaquín in the same building.

Fig. 7. Rue Schoelcher a short time before the tenement house was built where the Guilers rented their first separate apartment in Paris in 1925. After having moved in they learned that thousands of skeletons had been found during excavations to lay the foundations, skeletons of people massacred when the Paris Commune was crushed in 1871.

Fig. 8. 11 bis, rue Schoelcher today; the second of the two smaller windows in the middle is the one at which Anaïs is sitting on the cover photo, with Hugh standing below on the sidewalk.

Anaïs's and Hugh's dream flat was situated on the ground floor, with two big windows facing the Jewish corner of the cemetery, of which they only saw a bit of ivy-covered wall. On the ground floor was a big studio with an alcove, where they installed a small library, and a tiny, whitewashed kitchen. A staircase spiraled up to a bedroom and a bathroom. Anaïs, who all her life loved interior decorating, was soon busy collecting furniture and sewing pillowcases and curtains. When she had finished they went off on a late holiday to Touraine, and on their return to Paris in the autumn, Anaïs started to attend literature lectures at the Sorbonne.

In December 1925 John Erskine visited Paris with his wife and two children; Erskine was a professor of literature, as well as a writer and musician, who had been Hugh's teacher at Colombia University and later became a friend of the Guilers in New York. Both Hugh and Anaïs admired Erskine deeply, and Anaïs was very nervous before meeting him in Paris; what she really wished was that Erskine would be interested in her writing and encourage her to be a writer. Hugh showed selected parts of her diary to Erskine, who, to Anaïs's delight, found them both interesting and well-written.

On the surface it seemed that the situation had improved greatly for Anaïs, but she confides in her diary that she is almost constantly suffering from depression, a lack of self-confidence and a feeling that life is passing her by. She felt more and more lonely and isolated in Paris, which remained a nightmare to her. They socialized almost exclusively with Hugh's business friends. The worst thing was that Anaïs didn't even long for New York any longer, she just wanted to live somewhere "clean," where shameless eroticism was not in the air, where she wasn't followed by men murmuring disgusting invitations, and where couples in love didn't kiss openly in the streets. Young Anaïs had had a strict Catholic education, and it's no exaggeration to say that she suffered from sexual phobia. It seems probable from her writing that she may have remained a virgin during the first year of her marriage.

Her romantic cultural expectations were not met, either. During a holiday in Italy with Hugh in the spring of 1926, she complains in her diary: "Paris is old, envious of youth, an enemy of individualism, an enemy of mysticism, an enemy of energy" (*Early Diary 3*, p. 189).

The French cultural arrogance killed her inspiration and strangled all spontaneous creativity, and she shuddered at the thought of having to go back to Paris. In Italy Anaïs and Hugh decided after long discussions that they would return to New York after a year and put a stop to what they called their "European holiday."

But soon after returning to Paris they reversed their decision, due to a discovery they made in May 1926 and over which Anaïs quite unexpectedly exults in her diary. After a walk in the Luxemburg gardens, noisy and packed with people, she and Hugh asked the concierge if they could go onto the roof of their building to get some peace and enjoy the view. The concierge told them that the roof sloped and had no railings, but that there happened to be a small servant's room with a balcony and a nice view on the highest floor, with no tenant at present. Anaïs and Hugh were enchanted by the room and immediately rented it.

"We have no desire to return to New York," Anaïs writes in her diary in May 1926 (p. 205). The High Place, as they called it, became a sanctuary where Anaïs could spend her days writing in complete tranquility and to which only "significant people" would have access (p. 206).

At this point Anaïs decided to be "reasonable" about Paris. She had to endure it for the sake of Hugh, her mother and Joaquín. Meanwhile, she would make an effort to transform her "hate of Paris into writing and make it harmless," she writes in her diary in December 1926 (p. 248).

Unlike Anaïs, Hugh greatly appreciated life in Paris and regarded the French way of living as a challenge that stimulated his American fighting spirit. Although his job at the branch office in Paris meant reduced career opportunities, he very much wanted to stay there. In December 1926 his salary was substantially raised; his boss obviously wished to make it clear that he wouldn't like to lose the hardworking and popular Hugh Guiler. The First National Bank had its offices at 41, boulevard Haussmann; the building is still there, now occupied by a big department store.

In the summer of 1927 Anaïs and Hugh went on holiday to New York, where they met all their old friends and envied their American lifestyle. On the way back to Europe they were "so despondent that we wished that a storm might sink our ship" (p. 285). But having found Paris again Anaïs was amazed to discover that her attitude about the city had changed: after New York, Paris appeared as "very sweet, small, calm, wonderful," and she actually found herself looking forward to all the things waiting for her there. She and Hugh had started to make French friends, among them Hélène Boussinescq, a woman in her forties who was teaching English, translating English literature and socializing in literary circles. It was John Erskine who had introduced her to the Guilers during his visit to Paris in January 1926. At first Anaïs was a bit afraid of her resolute and cocksure manners, but gradually she began to appreciate "Boussie," who was to be their friend for many years.

In the autumn of 1927 Anaïs also started to take dancing lessons with the Spanish teacher Paco Miralles, whom she found "magical" and whose tenderness and humanity appeared to her as a contrast to the hard emotional coldness of the French. The training hall was situated at the corner of rue de Liège and rue de Clichy, a few blocks from Place de Clichy.

Anaïs loved these areas where, she writes, there was a bakery where she had coffee and a brioche, a bookshop where she borrowed modern books, and a jeweler who repaired her earrings and bracelets.

In the autumn of 1928, John Erskine returned to Paris with his family, this time for several months. The Guilers and the Erskines saw a lot of each other, and Anaïs became Erskine's guide to Paris. But in spite of all these activities and a growing circle of friends, Anaïs was restless and dissatisfied. In February 1929 she rages against herself in her diary: "I am now twenty-six and I have done nothing. No book, no stage career, a lot of unsatisfied wishes, and a realization that I am but half of what I hope to be" (*Early Diary 4*, p. 163).

Her relationship with her much-admired father figure John Erskine transformed into eroticism, but this experience also frustrated Anaïs: when they finally started a sexual affair in deepest secrecy it turned out that Erskine's virility failed. At the end of May 1929 he went back with his family to the U.S. and left Anaïs with a guilty conscience.

By now Hugh Guiler was earning so much money that they could afford to move to a bigger flat. With no premonitions whatsoever about the imminent stock exchange crash, they left rue Schoelcher on July 17, 1929, to install themselves in the fashionable 16th arrondissement at 47, boulevard Suchet, in a seven-room apartment which they were to share with Rosa and Joaquín.

Fig. 9. The entrance to 47, boulevard Suchet looks the same today as when the Guilers lived there.

Fig. 10. Interior of the apartment in boulevard Suchet, decorated by Anaïs in an Eastern style.

For several months, Anaïs was now busy arranging the new place. She put heart and soul into the work, and the result delighted so many of their circle of acquaintances that they asked her to decorate their homes, too, in her oriental-inspired style. But Anaïs was too busy: she continued her dancing lessons, worked on her novel and several short stories, and as well as that she had started to write an essay which Hugh read and corrected. This was not an altogether smooth collaboration since Anaïs was extremely sensitive to criticism.

November 1929 saw the crash of the New York stock exchange, and for a short time Hugh feared they would lose all their assets. They didn't at that point, but as the dollar plummeted Hugh's salary was reduced, and they had to live more modestly.

On March 8, 1930, Anaïs gave a dance performance at the Salle d'Iéna, an event that "le tout Paris" went to see. In the first row she thought she glimpsed her father, who had reason to be proud of his daughter that night: Anaïs and her teacher Miralles were very successful with their Spanish dances.

About a month later Anaïs writes in her diary that she is reading all the books of D. H. Lawrence, who had died on March 3, 1930. For Anaïs the news of his death came as a shock: she had written a letter to Lawrence that she had not yet mailed. Now she started to plan an essay about his work, with the provisional title "When D. H. Lawrence Found Himself." At the same time she worked on a novel, *Anita*, which she finished in May and let Hugh read. He was impressed.

The summer of 1930 was cold and rainy, and Anaïs, who felt the cold bitterly and who never got used to the Parisian climate, made fires well into June. The gloomy atmosphere wasn't improved by the fact that they gradually lost almost all their money in the wake of the big crash. Now all they had left was about 1,000 dollars, but they still didn't want to miss out on their holiday. In order to finance their summer trip to Caux in Normandy, a place Anaïs loved, they rented out their elegant apartment at boulevard Suchet through an agency and received 3,000 dollars, an enormous sum for then.

Fig. 11. Close to boulevard Suchet there was a small train station on the line circling the inner city of Paris, the Chemin de Fer de Ceinture; Anaïs must have taken the train many times from this station. The tracks are still there and a couple of times a year the old, now restored train is brought out for a run.

By now Anaïs had finished her essay on Lawrence, and in her diary she admits that France had done a lot for her intellectual development.

After the holiday Hugh and Anaïs had to leave the big apartment on boulevard Suchet, as they could no longer afford it. They decided to sublet it and look for a cheaper alternative. For Anaïs this was a hard blow, but she tried to hide her sorrow from Hugh.

"I will miss this place terribly," she writes in her diary in August 1930, "the energy and imagination I poured into it, the finality of it, the dreams I had of spending the rest of my life making it more beautiful..." (*Early Diary 4*, p. 322).

The search for a new place to live soon led the Guilers to an old house at 2 bis, rue de Montbuisson in Louveciennes, a village west of Paris, not far from Versailles. By renting the house in Louveciennes they would save 25,000 francs a year. On August 17, 1930, Hugh Guiler signed the contract, and in September they started to prepare for the move.

LOUVECIENNES

(1930 – 1936)

Reading Anaïs's description of Louveciennes and of the house at 2 bis, rue de Montbuisson at the beginning of *Diary 1* (1931-34), one hardly gets the impression that her heart had been filled with deep sorrow when she had been forced to move there. But *Diary 1* starts in the autumn of 1931, by which time Anaïs and Hugh had already lived in Louveciennes for one year, and Anaïs had arranged the house and garden the way she wanted. The rooms were painted in different warm colors, tile stoves had been installed, the fountain in front of the house was restored, and Anaïs had begun to realize that the calm life in Louveciennes was advantageous to a writer.

However, when the Guilers decided to move to Louveciennes, Anaïs was anything but happy. Not only had she had to leave her beloved, beautiful apartment on boulevard Suchet, but she had also had to leave the city for the countryside, and this in no way enchanted her. After so many difficult years Anaïs had finally begun to appreciate Paris. Her stubborn struggle to get something out of her life in Paris had finally yielded results, and at that point she saw herself forced to leave the city that at last had started to shimmer for her.

"I have less spirit to do the new place, less energy. I must make an effort," she writes in her diary in August 1930. "I had dreamed about being *near* everything. I am still so curious, so hungry, so restless, and I love the City" (*Early Diary*, p. 323).

Today you can reach Louveciennes via commuter train from Gare St-Lazare, and the trip through the suburban landscape takes half an hour. In Anaïs's era the trains didn't run as frequently as today, and the landscape they crossed was rural and idyllic.

"One hears the whistle of the small train from and to Paris. It is a train which looks ancient, as if it were still carrying the personages from Proust's novels to dine in the country," Anaïs writes in her diary (*Diary 1*, p. 5).

On September 27, 1930, Anaïs, assisted by her cousin Eduardo Sánchez, started to clean up the house in Louveciennes; it was in a deplorable state. They went there every day, tearing down spiders' webs and old wallpaper, plugging holes and preparing the walls for painting. The house in Louveciennes required "three times" as much work as the apartment at boulevard Suchet, "because the house was so old, so decrepit, so primitive in comfort, so dirty, so damp, so full of problems and obstacles," Anaïs writes in her diary in October 1930 (*Early Diary 4*, p. 351).

Anaïs and Eduardo must have worked hard, because as early as October 3, 1930 the Guilers were able to move in, together with Rosa, Joaquín and the Spanish maid Emilia, whom Henry Miller was always to call Amelia.

On October 16, the first room, Joaquín's studio, was finished; Anaïs had installed a fireplace and bookshelves and painted the room salmon pink. The curtains were to be turquoise. The whole house was to be painted in warm colors, as Anaïs writes in her diary: "...maids' room rose, my bedroom pale coral, dining room, as usual, deep coral. No more turquoise, because it's a cold color" (*Early Diary 4*, p. 352).

On the ground floor were the kitchen, the living room and the dining room. On the first floor were three rooms, and due to the slightly sloping ground the first floor became the ground floor at the back, facing onto an uncultivated garden behind the house. A small flight of stairs led to the second floor, consisting of one oblong room with a big pool table.

In the wing to the right, Rosa, Joaquín and Emilia were installed.

At the time I visited the mythical house at 2 bis, rue de Montbuisson, it was uninhabited and decrepit. The only hint of its former glory was a plaque on the pillar next to the front gate declaring that "Anaïs Nin, American novelist," lived there in the 1930s.

The owner, Monsieur Auzépy, maintained it, hoping that his children would take care of it when they inherited it. There was a new roof, and the rusty gate had just been replaced. Since then, the house has been sold and restored more than once.

Monsieur Auzépy bought the house at the beginning of the '60s, having rented it for many years as a summer and weekend house. He bought it from M. and Mme Leboeuf, who at that time lived in the house to the left of the gate, with direct entrance from the street, a property that Monsieur Auzépy also acquired later on.

Hugh Guiler signed the contract with Mme Emélie Leboeuf, who rented it after her parents' death. The Leboeufs lived in a big house at rue Renoir, only a block away.

Fig. 12. Gare St-Lazare, the station from which the train for Louveciennes still leaves.

After the war, Anaïs returned six times to Paris for short visits between 1958 and 1974. During one of these stays, in the spring of 1970, after the diaries had been published and were an international success, a

German TV team followed Anaïs wandering through her old haunts, including Louveciennes, where Monsieur Auzépy then happened to live permanently.

But when Anaïs walked up to the gate of 2 bis, rue de Montbuisson, she found it locked; neither she nor the TV team were admitted.

In fact, Monsieur Auzépy said that he was not opposed to letting Anaïs visit the mythical house, but when a person from the TV team had called him up, abruptly informing him that they were going to shoot Anaïs Nin's return to Louveciennes and ordered him to expect them at his house the next day, he had reacted in irritation. If the person who had called had only been reasonably polite, he claimed, he would have received Anaïs with pleasure.

At the beginning of the '80s, Hugh Guiler contacted Monsieur Auzépy, asking if he could come and see the house in Louveciennes during his imminent visit to Paris. Monsieur Auzépy, who then lived only periodically in Louveciennes, received the amiable Hugh Guiler, who thus revisited the house and garden after more than 45 years.

A year later Monsieur Auzépy also received Anaïs's brother, Joaquín, in Louveciennes. While the two of them walked in the garden at the back of the house, Joaquín stopped at the dried-up furrow that Anaïs describes as a brook in her diary, and Monsieur Auzépy asked him if there had ever been any water in it while they lived there.

"No," Joaquín answered smilingly. "But you see, Anaïs had such a lively imagination!"

Fig. 13. The station in Louveciennes at the beginning of the '30s.

Previous page:
Fig. 14. The Guilers' landlady, Madame Leboeuf, with her mother at the gate of the house at 2 bis, rue de Montbuisson in Louveciennes. The photograph was taken long before Anaïs and Hugh moved there.

Fig. 15. Monsieur Leboeuf at the same period.

Following page:
Fig. 16. This photograph of the house in Louveciennes was taken during the period when Anaïs and Hugh lived there. The paved front courtyard was then covered with gravel which crackled when Hugh arrived by car.

Fig. 17. 2 bis rue de Montbuisson in the mid-'90s.

Fig. 18. The Louveciennes house in the mid-'90s. There was no trace of the fountain.

Following Page:

Fig. 19. Madame Leboeuf with her mother sitting in a sofa in the garden behind the house. The photograph was probably taken between 1900-1910.

Previous page:
Fig. 20. The garden behind the house in the mid-'90s, at which time the white iron sofa in which Madame Leboeuf's mother sat was still there!

The name of Louveciennes, today a town of 8,000 inhabitants, was originally Mons Lupinus (Wolf Mountain), and its history is surprisingly interesting. Madame Du Barry, Louis XV's mistress, lived there for a while in a small château given to her by the king. Madame Du Barry was very fond of the castle and the village, but after the death of Louis XV in 1774, this paradise of hers was confiscated. Two years later, however, she was back at Louveciennes, having successfully persuaded Louis XVI to allow her to be reinstalled in her beloved rural château. The villagers greeted her enthusiastically; she was well liked, above all because she helped the poor. Her friend, the painter Elisabeth Vigée Lebrun, visited her several times and also did her portrait there.

During the terror of the French revolution, Madame Du Barry was arrested at Louveciennes. According to hearsay, she was imprisoned for a couple of days in the house at 2 bis, rue de Montbuisson, before she was brought to Paris, where she was executed in September 1793. Before that, her lover, the Duke du Brissac, had been guillotined, and there were rumors that his head was thrown over the wall of Madame Du Barry's property, a story that Anaïs told Henry Miller. Whether true or not is uncertain, but somebody's head must have been thrown into the château grounds, because about two hundred years later a human skull was found during roadwork in a place that had formerly belonged to the castle.

Elisabeth Vigée Lebrun, who fled to England and Switzerland during the revolution, returned to France in 1809 and bought a house in Louveciennes, where she died in 1841. She is buried in the local cemetery.

During the latter part of the 19th century many future painters sought out Louveciennes during briefer or longer periods. The young Claude Monet, Alfred Sisley and Pierre-Auguste Renoir all worked as apprentices in an established artist's studio there, before they left together to roam about the countryside, convinced that they would never revolutionize art if they remained in conventional, more conservative studios. Later Camille Pissarro settled down in Louveciennes, and Claude Monet visited him over a couple of winters. Monet stored some 200 canvases there that disappeared during the German occupation.

While busily preparing for the move from Paris to Louveciennes, Anaïs took time off to visit the editor Edward Titus, above all to try to interest him in her short stories. The Polish-born Titus had come to Paris after World War I with his wife Helena Rubinstein. Fairly soon the couple got divorced, but they stayed in touch. In 1924, Titus opened a small rare bookshop at 4, rue Delambre in Montparnasse, close to Le Dôme. Two years later he started a publishing house for English and American literature, the Black Manikin Press.

Fig. 21. The Louveciennes château as it looked at the time of Anaïs. In the 1990s, it was abandoned by its owner, a phony Japanese businesswoman; it has since been sold and carefully restored.

In 1928, Titus had also acquired the literary magazine *This Quarter*, which published poetry, prose and criticism by English-speaking writers living in Paris. (It was thanks to *This Quarter* that Anaïs discovered the psychoanalyst Otto Rank, who was to be so important to her some years later, both intellectually and emotionally.) Titus was the first to publish D. H. Lawrence's *Lady Chatterley's Lover* in 1929. Lawrence had first turned to Sylvia Beach of the bookshop Shakespeare & Co. with his controversial novel, but Beach was busy acting as James Joyce's European editor, a heroic mission, reason enough not to take on another problematic writer. Furthermore, Beach didn't like *Lady Chatterley*, but she diplomatically kept silent about that and put Lawrence in touch with Edward Titus.

Titus, who lived in an elegant little flat above his bookshop, found Anaïs Nin's writings promising, but he didn't accept any of her short stories for publication. He wanted her to rewrite them, remove superfluous adjectives and improve the transitions. Before contacting Titus, Anaïs had, on several occasions, sent short stories to Beach, who answered imperturbably that she was too busy editing James Joyce to read other writers' works.

The magazine *The Canadian Forum*, however, accepted Anaïs's essay on Lawrence. It was published in October 1930, unpaid and under a pseudonym. It might have been this event that encouraged Anaïs to get in touch with Titus once more, in January 1931. This time she casually mentioned that she had written a book about D. H. Lawrence simply to gauge Titus's reaction. "His ears pricked up," she writes in her diary. "He had a publisher just longing for a book on Lawrence" (*Early Diary 4*, p. 379).

Fig. 22. Rue Delambre in the '20s. Today Edward Titus's bookshop, no. 4, is a fish shop.

It seems that Titus didn't publish many books himself, but acted mainly as a literary agent, only financing the publication of valuable works no other publisher would take on and in which he really believed.

Stimulated by Titus's interest, Anaïs started to expand her essay about Lawrence into a book, working obsessively. At the same time one of her short stories, "A Waste of Timelessness," was accepted by *La Nouvelle Revue*.

Having worked nonstop for sixteen days, Anaïs finally finished her book about Lawrence.

"It's more or less *done*," she writes in her diary on January 23, 1931. "22,500 words—needs revising, some details, but the big, important things are in. I cannot believe it. Throughout, I have been astonishingly sure and confident" (p. 379).

As soon as the book was ready, Anaïs went to Paris to give it to Titus, who decided to publish it after having had it revised by a collaborator.

In May 1931 Anaïs visited Shakespeare & Co. for the first time, at 12, rue de l'Odéon, and registered as a member. The small bookshop was already a legend. The young Sylvia Beach had started it in 1919 on rue Duputryen, as a combined bookshop/library. Two years later Shakespeare & Co. moved to rue de l'Odéon, where it rapidly became a meeting place for English-speaking writers such as James Joyce, Gertrude Stein and Ernest Hemingway; French writers interested in Anglo-Saxon literature were also part of the circle around Beach. When Anaïs came to register, Beach immediately felt sympathetic towards the frail, dark young woman who she thought looked Japanese.

The first book that Anaïs borrowed at Shakespeare & Co. was e. e. cummings' *enormous rooms*. The aversion she had felt towards modern literature when arriving in Paris six years earlier, when she had read classics almost exclusively, was by now completely eroded, and her interest in modern literature and art flared up passionately.

Fig. 23. Place de l'Odéon, where rue de l'Odéon starts. Sylvia Beach's bookshop Shakespeare & Co. was situated a few blocks farther down on the left, at no. 12. Today a women's apparel shop occupies the legendary premises.

During the summer of 1931, Anaïs and Hugo spent a couple weeks in Majorca, and during the autumn they once more visited the U.S., where they met the Erskines, among others. Anaïs was still attracted to John Erskine, but during the stay in New York her feelings for him cooled considerably, especially since the conservative Erskine attacked James Joyce and Anaïs's beloved and admired D. H. Lawrence, and worse still criticized a novel that Anaïs had finished and brought for him to read, *The Woman No Man Could Hold* (never published).

Upon returning to Paris the proofs of the book on Lawrence awaited Anaïs. Rumors about it had already started to circulate before publication in the literary circles of Montparnasse. A person named Henry Miller had had a chance to read the manuscript, thanks to his friend Richard Galen Osborn, an American lawyer with literary ambitions and a bohemian temperament. Osborn worked for the First National Bank, where he had met Hugh Guiler. Hugh, who was proud of his wife's literary talents, had probably told Osborn that Edward Titus would publish Anaïs's book on Lawrence, and Osborn arranged for Miller to read the manuscript. Henry Miller was very impressed and curious to meet the unknown young writer of the original and empathetic analysis. In this way, it was D. H. Lawrence, who had died in March 1930 in a sanatorium in Vence in southern France, who brought Anaïs Nin and Henry Miller together and who symbolized the profound common denominator between them that no one in their acquaintance could quite fathom, least of all Hugh.

Fig. 24. Henry Miller in Paris, with the bicycle he bought after having moved to Clichy.

Henry Miller first arrived in Paris in April 1928 at the age of 37 with his then wife June. June had already been to Paris in 1927, and on her return to New York she was enthusiastic: she said she had met the likes of Ossip Zadkine, Marcel Duchamp and Edgar Varèse, whom Henry hadn't known of, and she asserted that Paris was the right place for him to be. When June had raised enough money a year later, she went back to Paris with Henry, but he was not as delighted with Paris as June had thought he would be. This might have been due to the fact that many Americans were leaving Paris towards the end of the '20s, when the atmosphere was growing increasingly xenophobic. In August 1927, furious French demonstrators had stormed the American embassy and attacked Americans in the bars of Montparnasse after the news that the anarchists Sacco and Vanzetti had been executed in the U.S. It's not improbable that Henry and June were influenced by the atmosphere of Montparnasse at that time; after only a couple of weeks they rented bicycles and spent the rest of the year discovering the countryside.

One year later, in March 1930, Henry returned to Paris, alone, persuaded by June to go back there in order to write. She also promised to send him money. As a matter of fact, Henry had wished to travel on to Madrid, but he was now stranded with no money in Paris, where June's promised checks arrived only sporadically. Soon he couldn't afford even a simple hotel room and had to live from hand to mouth, relying on the good will of others. Often he spent the night at some of the big Montparnasse brasseries, preferably La Coupole, where one could sit the night with only a cup of coffee and where the establishment even provided writing paper. It was in the cafés of Montparnasse that Henry Miller got to know the big foreign colony in Paris and met people who helped him out. For some time he stayed at the flat of the writer Michael Fraenkel at 18, Villa Seurat, to which he was to return several years later when Anaïs managed to rent a studio there after his move from Clichy.

At Le Dôme in Montparnasse, Henry Miller bumped into Alfred Perlès, whose acquaintance he had made in Paris the first time with June and who now became a friend. Perlès had mercy on the homeless Miller and let him live for a while secretly in his room on the fifth floor of the Hôtel Central, 1 bis, rue du Maine in Montparnasse. Fred, who worked nights at the *Chicago Tribune*, finished at around two in the morning, when Henry would be waiting for him in a café. Then they would walk together to the cheap Hôtel Central, where there was no reception; one just pressed a button and waited for the door to open automatically. As he passed the janitor's little window, Fred only had to shout his name and room number and Henry could sneak upstairs with him, unnoticed. This went on for several weeks. In the morning Fred would leave some money on the mantelpiece so that Henry could have breakfast when he awoke. Then he spent the whole day and half of the night wandering about Paris. Most often he explored the city alone, but sometimes he bumped into other wanderers, such as the photographer Brassaï or the American journalist Wambly Bald, and joined them.

Fig. 25. Hôtel Central, where Anaïs started her passionate affair with Henry Miller, is still to be found at 1 bis, rue du Maine in Montparnasse.

Brassaï met Henry Miller for the first time in December 1930, at Le Dôme. "I will never forget that rosy face sticking up from a crumpled raincoat," Brassaï writes in his *Henry Miller grandeur nature*, where he describes Miller as a curious and attentive man, with a touch of the wise Tibetan. According to Brassaï, Miller loved the Parisian pissoirs that "made his eyes fill with tears of happiness." He would walk a long way just to visit his favorite pissoirs, including the one at the corner of rue St-Jacques and rue Abbé de l'Epée, in front of a school for the deaf and dumb. The school is still there, but the pissoirs no longer remain. By the '30s the municipal authorities had already started to remove numerous pissoirs, realizing that they were meeting points for homosexuals.

Wambly Bald, who wrote about Montparnassian life for the *Chicago Tribune*, dedicated an article of October 14, 1931, to his first meeting with Henry Miller, who by now was known in the bars around Vavin. According to certain sources, it was Henry Miller himself who wrote the article, in which Bald tells how a lonely man started to follow him one evening not far from the Louvre:

Fig. 26. View from the fifth floor of the Hôtel Central over the small park that Henry Miller was very fond of.

Following page:
Fig. 27. Rue Scribe, where American Express is still situated in the big building to the left, at no. 11.

"He wore corduroy pants and a grey jacket and thick glasses. His hat was nonchalantly pushed down askew and the exposed side of his head was totally bald. It was Henry Miller, the novelist."

Miller caught up with Bald, introduced himself as out of work and broke, but emphasized that Montparnasse was a fabulous place where he always bumped into people who were prepared to help him.

"Miller is a true child of Montparnasse, the salt of the block," Bald/Miller wrote, and before they parted that evening Bald dug some money out of his pocket and told Henry to go and have a meal.

During Henry Miller's first vagabond year in Paris his address was the American Express at 11, rue Scribe, not far from the Place de l'Opéra, where he went several times a week to pick up his mail and occasionally a modest check from June. Situated close to the American Express was the *Chicago Tribune*, at 5, rue Lamartine, in a block milling with prostitutes and pimps, much to Henry's delight. Opposite the newspaper was the Hôtel Cronstadt, where Henry put up every now and then when he could afford it; he was very fond of this, in his eyes, so typically French hotel.

In the autumn of 1931, Richard Osborn appeared on the scene. Henry Miller had met him at the American Club, and when Osborn heard that he was broke and almost down and out he brought him to his flat at 2, rue Auguste Bartholdi, where he stayed for an extended time. Miller returned Osborn's generosity by cleaning up, making the fire and cooking. He spent the rest of his time writing, above all long and detailed letters to his closest friends in America about Paris and his experiences there, letters that were later to be the basis of *Tropic of Cancer*.

The small street Auguste-Bartholdi, two minutes from the Dupleix metro, is still intact; opposite number 2 is one of the few Parisian bars that have kept their original décor, including its formerly typical zinc counter. At that counter Henry Miller must have stood with his morning coffee many times.

In December 1931 Henry Miller was invited to lunch at the Guilers' in Louveciennes courtesy of Richard Osborn. In her diary Anaïs says that she got in touch with Osborn since she had to ask a lawyer for advice concerning her contract with Titus. She describes Osborn as a bohemian who spent his nights in Montparnasse and arrived at the office in the morning with his suit stained and crumpled. Osborn had two favorite monologues, one about an imaginary court case, the other about his friend Henry Miller, who was writing a giant novel about all the things that other writers omitted, breaking all taboos.

Osborn had shown Anaïs an article that Miller had recently written about Luis Buñuel's film *L'Âge d'Or*, published in *The New Review*, a literary magazine owned by Titus's rival Samuel Putnam (Putnam had earlier published *This Quarter* together with Titus, but after a dispute he started his own magazine). Anaïs was thoroughly enthusiastic about Henry Miller's essay on Buñuel:

"There is in this piece of writing a primitive, savage quality...the words are slung like axes, explode with hatred, and it was like hearing wild drums in the midst of the Tuileries," she writes in her diary (*Diary 1*, p. 7).

Shortly afterwards Henry Miller received an invitation for lunch in Louveciennes. Osborn dined in Louveciennes on November 30, 1931, and returned for lunch next day with his much talked-of friend Miller.

By now, Anaïs had lived at 2 bis, rue de Montbuisson in Louveciennes for more than a year and had had a lot of time to add her distinct character to the house. She had lived through a summer with her honeysuckle-scented garden that she had tidied up but left wild and enticing at the back of the house. Her nostalgia for Paris and the apartment at boulevard Suchet had faded away, and she had started to appreciate life in Louveciennes. She was therefore feeling at ease in her new home when Henry Miller stepped out of the car on the gravel drive in front of the house and walked up to her. Henry was certainly interested in meeting the writer of the essay on Lawrence, but even more than that he was looking forward to a fine, free meal.

"When he first stepped out of the car and walked towards the front door where I stood waiting, I saw a man I liked. In his writing he is flamboyant, virile, animal, magnificent. He's a man whom life makes drunk, I thought. He is like me," Anaïs writes after her first meeting with Henry (*Henry and June*, p. 6).

Only a couple of days later Henry took the small train to Louveciennes to meet Anaïs again and continue his discussion with her: she had promised to read an excerpt from her diary to him and he had promised to bring the beginning of the manuscript that was to become *Tropic of Cancer*. After only the second meeting Anaïs already writes in her diary that Henry Miller is a man whom she could love.

A few weeks after Anaïs and Henry had met, Henry's beautiful, mythomaniac wife, June, unexpectedly ambled into Paris. Anaïs immediately invited the Millers to Louveciennes, where they had a New Year's Eve dinner. Before the imminent meeting with Anaïs, of whom Henry had talked so enthusiastically, June had dressed up provocatively in a purple velvet dress with holes at the elbows, a heavy cape and a dirty hat.

"I wanted to look like a tramp. I wanted to provoke, I wanted to bring Henry back to reality..." June said later. Her attitude seems to have been skeptical. Why would a cultivated upper class couple invite two broke bohemians to dinner?

The Millers were fetched at the station in Louveciennes by Hugh's driver in a limousine. During the evening June's skepticism was transformed into delight, and Anaïs found herself as attracted to June as she was to Henry. At the end of the evening, she writes in her diary that she was in love with June, who was the most beautiful woman she had ever seen. Until June returned to New York at the end of January 1932, she and Anaïs saw a lot of each other.

Before leaving Paris, June met Wambly Bald, who dedicated an article to her in the *Chicago Tribune* of January 12, 1932. He describes June as a born actress, making her entry at Le Select, powdered in white and with her "awe-inspiring beauty" immediately finding her audience. She spoke with a drawling, hypnotic voice and created an atmosphere of unreality around her.

Nobody knew the real color of her hair, as she regularly dyed it. Presently it was a golden rusty red. She confided to Bald that she "aroused peoples' slumbering vices" and that they hated her for that. She talked about her earlier experiences in Paris, how she snubbed Cocteau and Picasso and called them impostors, how she swam naked in the Seine and was arrested. Now she was in Paris for the fourth time. Every time she came to the city the most amazing things happened.

Although June perfectly fit into the bohemian life of Montparnasse, she soon returned to the U.S., leaving Henry to Anaïs. As soon as she had left, Anaïs invited Henry to Louveciennes; they both needed to discuss their feelings for June.

"We walked off our restlessness, and we talked. This is in both of us an obsession to grasp June. He has no jealousy of me, because he said that I brought out wonderful things in June, that it was the first time that June had *ever* attached herself to a woman of value," Anaïs writes in her diary in January 1932 (*Henry and June*, p. 33).

Thanks to Hugh, the broke and homeless Henry Miller found employment as a *répétiteur d'anglais*—conversation teacher—at the Lycée Carnot in Dijon, within the framework of a French-American project.

When Henry left for Dijon, Anaïs sought refuge in Switzerland where she traveled alone in order to analyze her feelings, above all for June. It was now that Anaïs and Henry started their correspondence that was to continue for the rest of their lives, even if the intensity faded over the years.

Henry felt ill at ease in Dijon, but the gloomy town gave him excellent material for *Tropic of Cancer*, in which he describes it as a kind of limbo. He had plenty of time to write; the lessons were few and didn't require any preparations. Henry improvised and the pupils appreciated his performance. Even though the food in the staff dining room was dull and the wine wretched, Henry was served three meals a day and didn't have to spend valuable time keeping hunger at bay. So he endured it, although he didn't get the salary he was promised and worked merely for bed and board. On hearing this Anaïs was very upset and thought that Henry ought to break his contract, but Henry preferred the dullness of Dijon to his uncertain existence in Paris.

As a reward for his stoicism he quite unexpectedly got a letter in February from Fred Perlès, saying that he had found a job for him at the *Chicago Tribune*. In a letter dated February 21, 1932, Henry wrote ecstatically to Anaïs (who was by then back in Louveciennes) that he would soon return to Paris: "I have received a telegram and a letter from my friend Fred saying that the editor offered me a permanent job on the *Tribune* as assistant finance editor. Salary to start 1,200 frs a month (*pas beaucoup!*) but a chance for an increase soon. The hours are from 8:30 p.m. to 1 a.m. (my hours) and the work is easy" (*A Literate Passion*, p. 11).

It actually sounds a bit strange that the *Chicago Tribune* would employ a shiftless writer with no money on its financial staff, and indeed the work turned out to be proofreading.

Previous page:
Fig. 28. Anaïs Nin in the garden in Louveciennes at the beginning of the '30s.

As soon as Henry was back in Paris, where he put up at the Hôtel Central at 1 bis, rue du Maine, he wanted to see Anaïs, but at the lovely house in Louveciennes a full tempest was blasting. On February 26, 1932, Anaïs writes in a letter to Henry, for the first time addressed to the *Chicago Tribune*, that "unfortunately we won't be able to meet on Sunday" as planned, because Rosa was so upset about her daughter's "obscene" essay on D. H. Lawrence, just published, that she wanted to move from Louveciennes immediately, principally to protect Joaquín from Anaïs's bad influence (*A Literate Passion*, p. 15). On Sunday, Hugh and Anaïs were to go to Paris to look at a flat for Rosa and Joaquín to rent. However, the tumult doesn't seem to have lasted long, because Rosa and Joaquín didn't move to Paris until the following year.

Fig. 29. 5, rue Lamartine, where Henry worked for a brief period as proofreader at the Chicago Tribune. Today a branch of the French tax bureau occupies the premises.

Fig. 30. Opposite the Chicago Tribune stood, and still stands, one of Henry Miller's favorite hotels, the Hôtel Cronstadt, 10, rue Lamartine.

At the beginning of March, Anaïs and Henry were finally reunited. They met at Café Chez les Vikings at 29-31, rue Vavin, not far from the Hôtel Central. Today the building at rue Vavin is newly restored, but there is no longer any café there.

On March 4, 1932, Henry wrote a letter to Anaïs from the Café Vikings, only a couple of minutes after she had left him: "No, I can't restrain it. I tell you what you already know—I love you," he exclaims as an opening (*A Literate Passion*, p. 16).

His feelings for her, stirred into being from the very first moment, had only grown during the period they were apart, and now he felt he had to share them with her. He writes that he is "continually on the point of throwing my arms around you" and that while he wanted to take her back to his room, "it seemed so sordid, leading you back to my miserable hotel" (pp. 16, 17).

Two days later he writes again, from the hotel, at half past one in the morning. The work at the newspaper, which he had figured would be easy, turned out to be quite arduous, and Henry is "dizzy, dizzy, I tell you" (p. 18).

It's obvious from Anaïs's letter to Henry of March 9, 1932 that they have by now embarked on their love affair, in the very room at Hôtel Central that Henry was so ashamed of. Both were deeply affected by the experience.

A couple of days later Henry writes a long letter to Anaïs, telling her about a move to a flat at 4, avenue Anatole France in Clichy, which he is to share with Fred Perlès. They had realized that they could rent a whole flat with a bathroom and a kitchen in the working suburb of Clichy at the same price they paid for their respective rooms at Hôtel Central.

The tenement house that Henry and Fred moved to was newly built, in Art Deco style. In 1915, the municipality of Clichy had already embarked on an enterprise to clear some appallingly decrepit blocks and build houses intended for poor families with numerous children, but the project never quite worked out. After the war a new institution took over, the *Office Publique d'Habitation à Bon Marché*, aiming at constructing cheap housing; it was this public office that started to build a number of tenement houses on avenue Anatole France (not to be confused with the street with the same name in Paris). The first of these aesthetically pleasing rows of tenement houses was finished in 1928. Number 4 was ready to receive its new inhabitants in 1930.

It's not impossible that Henry got the idea of renting a flat in Clichy because he knew that Louis-Ferdinand Céline, whom he admired immensely, lived and worked there as a physician to the poor.

Céline's novel *Voyage au bout de la nuit*, which was to create such enormous excitement, had not yet been published, but according to Brassaï, Henry had already read the manuscript in 1931, thanks to Céline's literary agent, and had told his friends that no other writer had impressed him in such a shocking way.

However, Céline had recently moved to Montmartre, but he went on working every day at his dispensary in Clichy, and Henry might have been hoping to bump into him.

Fig. 31. Place de Clichy, from which runs rue de Clichy, a street that Anaïs was especially fond of. To the left in the photograph is Wepler, a café that was a favorite of Henry Miller when he lived in Clichy.

In the early '30s, the last station on the metro was Porte de Clichy; today the line has been extended to Asnier-Gennevilliers, on the Seine. From Porte de Clichy it took around twenty minutes to reach avenue Anatole France on foot. You had to cross insecure blocks, and Fred, always prepared for an attack on his way home after working late, went armed with a knife; Henry trusted his heavy Mexican stick, one of the few things he had brought from New York.

Anaïs describes the flat at 4, avenue Anatole France as rather gloomy, with no curtains in the kitchen windows which overlooked a small back street of ugly houses. Fred found the view from the kitchen window equally depressing, after the magnificent view from the fifth floor of the Hôtel Central.

Charmless or not, from now on Anaïs and Henry had a place where they could meet in relative privacy. Anaïs would tell Hugh that she was going to Clichy where she and Henry worked together on their manuscripts, which was in fact a half-truth. After having read the unfinished *Tropic of Cancer* with delight and admiration, Anaïs now dedicated herself to revising his text and offering constructive suggestions for improvement. Henry in turn examined Anaïs's writings and commented upon them. Both were outsiders and found in each other the much longed-for support and commitment they so needed.

Previous page:
Fig. 32. Avenue Anatole France in Clichy; the photo was taken in 1932, the same year as Henry Miller and Fred Perlès moved into no. 4 at the beginning of the street on the right, when the beautiful tenement houses in Art Deco style were newly built.

During the eventful month of March 1932, Anaïs went to a small hotel with her cousin Eduardo Sánchez for a first—and last—erotic encounter. As a young girl Anaïs had been hopelessly in love with the handsome Eduardo; though he was homosexual, her feelings were returned, although the pair never before had an affair.

Eduardo Sánchez moved to Paris at the beginning of the '30s and started psychoanalysis with Doctor René Allendy, the founder of the French Psychoanalytical Society. During his analysis, Eduardo told Allendy that he was still in love with Anaïs, to him the ideal woman. Anaïs consented to the amorous meeting mostly through compassion, hoping that it would boost Eduardo's virility and self-confidence, but she had no plans to repeat the experience.

Fig. 33. Daily life in Clichy in the '20s, rue de Neuilly. Henry was to always prefer working-class areas, while Anaïs was drawn to the more fashionable districts.

Previous page:
Fig. 34. The small back street one could see from the kitchen window of Henry's and Fred's flat in Clichy (pictured above) is still there.

Fig. 35. 32, rue Blondel, where Anaïs and Hugh visited a brothel recommended to them by Henry. The street is still a hangout for prostitutes.

In March 1932, Anaïs also visited a brothel at 32, rue Blondel, a few blocks from Porte St-Martin and the metro station of Strasbourg-St-Denis, a place that Henry was well acquainted with. In the expurgated diary she states that she went there with Henry in February, but in *Henry and June* we read that she went there with Hugh, after Henry had recommended it to them. Hugh and Anaïs watched a lesbian show in a small, private room and returned happily to Louveciennes, where Hugh "adored my body because it was lovelier than what he had seen and we sank into sensuality with new realization" (*Henry and June*, p. 72).

Fig. 36. Porte St-Martin, close to rue Blondel.

Henry's job as a proofreader at the *Chicago Tribune* lasted only a few months; it seems that his application for a work permit was turned down and he had to leave, much to Anaïs's relief. On several occasions in her diary she expresses her worries about Henry's sensitive eyes that would start to run in smoky rooms and were now overworked by exacting proofreading. In any case, the experience at the *Chicago Tribune* gave further material for *Tropic of Cancer*, where Henry describes how proofreading quickly made him immune to all disasters and sufferings in the world, and how all events, enormous or petty, horrendous or trivial, end up at the same entropic level for the proofreader.

In April 1932, Anaïs visited Dr. René Allendy for the first time, "to talk about Eduardo." Eduardo had confided his erotic adventure with Anaïs to Allendy and was now unable to accept that it was never to be repeated. On meeting Allendy, a tall, patriarchal man with a beard, Anaïs also told him about the tragedy she had experienced because of her father, who had never shown any affection for her and who had abandoned Rosa and the three children when Anaïs was ten. The fatherly Allendy inspired confidence and soon became her analyst. At the beginning Anaïs talked almost exclusively about her affair with Henry, a relationship Allendy disapproved of.

As her feelings for Henry intensified, her relationship with Hugh deteriorated. When one day in April Henry openly asked her what she got from her marriage with the nice, friendly Hugh, who according to Henry was inferior to Anaïs in every way, she broke down and started to cry.

Previous page:
*Fig. 37. 67, rue de l'Assomption, where the psychiatrist René Allendy lived and worked. "Doctor Allendy's private house, three floors, with a small front garden and a back garden, a kitchen in the basement, his office and parlor on the first floor, bedrooms on the second floor, resembles the house in Brussels where we lived when I was eight and nine years old," Anaïs writes in her diary in April 1932 (*Diary 1, p. 95*). Today the house is squeezed in between two modern buildings.*

"My life is a mess," she confessed (*Henry and June*, p. 140). She found it increasingly difficult to bear Hugh's sexual urges; the only person she longed for was Henry. Her sexual passion was now growing into a deep love. As for Henry, he had been in love from the very beginning. As if life weren't complicated enough Anaïs started to flirt with Allendy, who rose to the bait with seemingly no professional qualms; at the end of June he kissed her for the first time, and she was intent on continuing her flirtation with her analyst.

In July 1932 Anaïs secretly underwent plastic surgery to correct the tip of her nose; after the surgery she went to the Tyrol, where she was to spend the holiday with Hugh. During these summer weeks she felt unexpectedly close to Hugh. She writes in her diary that she is strangely indifferent to Henry's long, passionate letters and feels a desperate need of Allendy in her confusion.

Allendy's unprofessional jealousy towards Henry Miller had grown during the summer. He continued his physical approaches, encouraged by Anaïs.

"We kiss more warmly than the last time. Henry is still between me and a full tasting of Allendy, but the deviltry in me is stronger," she writes in her diary in September 1932 (*Henry and June*, pp. 243-244).

She also persuaded Hugh to begin analysis with Allendy, hoping that Allendy would "teach him how to be less dependent on me for his happiness" (p. 246).

In autumn 1932 Henry Miller got in touch with William Bradley, a literary agent in Paris who succeeded in getting editor Jack Kahane interested in *Tropic of Cancer*. Kahane had left England in the '20s and settled down in Paris, where he founded Obelisk Press at the beginning of the '30s in order to publish his own books and valuable works that wouldn't pass British and American censorship. Kahane wanted to publish *Tropic of Cancer* but was not prepared to pay for the printing of the book. Anaïs promised Henry to raise money, somehow; she probably thought she could persuade Hugh to pay for the publishing of Henry's novel, but as it turned out she had reached her affectionate and tolerant husband's limit, and he didn't think much of Henry Miller anyway. (It would take another two years before Kahane published the book, and even then it was thanks to Anaïs, who had finally managed to borrow money from her next psychoanalyst, Otto Rank.)

Both Henry and Anaïs knew that sooner or later they would have to cope with the problem of June; they just didn't know when and how. But in October 1932 June arrived in Paris, as unexpectedly as she had in December the previous year, replacing Anaïs in Henry's bed at avenue Anatole France in Clichy. Both Anaïs and Henry felt strongly about June, as strongly as they felt about each other. Thus, conflict seemed inevitable.

This complicated situation came to a head in November, when June realized that Anaïs had become Henry's mistress in her absence. From that moment June's went into a vengeful fury, threatening to kill both Anaïs and Henry. Anaïs felt reasonably safe in Louveciennes, but she worried about Henry and gave him money to go to London when the conflict reached its peak in December 1932. Before he left, however, June turned up in Clichy and claimed the money for herself.

Upon hearing this, Anaïs immediately urged Henry to get out of harm's way in Louveciennes, where he stayed for a couple of days, while his faithful friend Fred raised new money for the trip to London. But this time Henry was stopped by British Customs in Newhaven, where they thought he looked shabby and had too little cash; after a night in custody he was sent back across the channel. (This tragicomedy is described in Miller's short story "Via Dieppe-Newhaven," included in *Max and the White Phagocytes*.)

When Henry returned to Paris, crestfallen, June had already left. June Edith Smith-Miller thereby disappeared forever from Henry's and Anaïs's lives, at least physically. Henry and June obtained their divorce in Mexico at the end of 1934.

After these dramatic events Henry took refuge in Louveciennes, where Hugh soon started to wonder how long "that Henry" was planning to stay. But it was ironically Hugh who had to go away for ten days to see his family who lived in London, and Henry could safely enjoy Christmas in Louveciennes with Anaïs, knowing that the maid Emilia would never tell Hugh about it. The intense relationship between Anaïs and Henry peaked during those days. On Christmas Day 1932 Anaïs writes in her diary: "Only Henry and I, working together in the stillness of Louveciennes. The church bells tolling. The serenity of knowing what is supremely and divinely right. The world is at last focused. This is the center... On Christmas night the moon shone full, and that alone is holy; for that alone the bells should toll, and music should rise, and mouse-stepped people climb cathedral steps; for the miracle of the great rounded fullness between man and woman, for the miracle of totality" (*Incest*, pp. 77-78).

But not even this deeply experienced fullness could stop Anaïs from continuing her flirtation with Allendy. In April 1933 she accompanied her psychoanalyst to a hotel room on rue de la Boule Rouge, close to the Folies Bergères, where she became his mistress. Despite of her disillusionment at Allendy's sexual performance, she agreed to return to the same hotel with him after he had promised that he would punish her next time for playing with men's feelings, a promise that Anaïs found exciting. But not even his using a whip transformed Allendy into a fierce lover. "I was fucked by death," Anaïs writes in her diary (p. 149).

Previous page:
Fig. 38. The garden with sculptures in front of the Zadkine museum at 100, rue d'Assas.

In February 1933 Anaïs met the Russian sculptor Ossip Zadkine, who arrived in France before World War I. In 1928 he managed to rent two small houses with a garden at 100, rue d'Assas, a few blocks from the boarding house where Anaïs and Hugh lived in 1925. Zadkine invited her to his studio in one of the houses; in the other house he lived with his wife, Valentine Praz. The yard was filled with his statues. In her diary, Nin says, "There are so many of them that they look like a forest, as if so many trees had been growing there and he had carved them into a forest of bodies, faces, animals," Anaïs writes in her diary after her first meeting with Zadkine in 1933 (*Diary 1*, p. 178).Today the studio has been transformed into the Musée Zadkine; the forest of sculptures is still there, the same as Anaïs last saw it.

In March 1933, Allendy introduced Anaïs to Antonin Artaud, the French surrealist poet, theatre theoretician and actor, who immediately fascinated her and by whom she was subsequently seduced. However, it turned out that Artaud also lacked potency, which led to conflict.

Anaïs took refuge on the Riviera, where she was to see her father. Through a friend, he, Joaquín Nin Sr, let Anaïs know that he mourned his lost daughter and yearned to get her back. During their time together they embarked on an incestuous affair, described in detail in the unexpurgated diary entitled *Incest*. After this shattering experience, Anaïs had difficulties resuming her affair with Henry. Rather early on she told him about it, however, and this seems to have had a therapeutic effect: at the beginning of August she is already writing in her diary: "Everything with Henry as before. No alteration in our passion or in our talks" (*Incest*, p. 236).

Anaïs went on spending much of her time in Clichy, where she was working on her poetic novella that she first entitled "Alraune," later to be published under the title of *The House of Incest*.

During the autumn of 1933 Anaïs often visited her father and his young wife Maruca at 27, rue Henri Heine, not far from Allendy's house. She also took up analysis again with Allendy for a brief period, but nothing indicates that she told him about her incestuous experience.

In order to be "absolved" for her illicit love, she had to find another analyst. In November 1933 she contacted Otto Rank. Both Anaïs and Henry had read about the important role played by neurosis in creative activity in Rank's book, *Art and Artist*, which was to become something of a house bible to them and to many intellectuals of that generation.

Otto Rank had moved from Vienna to Paris in 1926 with his wife and daughter, after a schism with Freud and the Freudian psychoanalytical establishment. He lectured at the Sorbonne and received patients in his apartment at 9, rue Louis Boilly.

Rank advised Anaïs to stop writing her diary, which he considered her "last defense against analysis," and which Anaïs herself called her "opium." He also wanted her to leave home for a period and stop seeing

Henry, simply concentrating on analysis. Anaïs didn't mind leaving Hugh and Louveciennes for a while, and she stayed in a hotel at 26, rue des Marronniers in the 16th arrondissement, not far from Allendy, where she also rented a room for Henry, behind Rank's back. She had chosen the hotel because it was modern and elegant without being extravagant. It would soon turn out that she and Henry lived in a hotel that was "well known for temporary alliances, well-kept mistresses, intended to give the illusion of home," Anaïs writes in *Incest* in November 1933, adding that this suited her perfectly (pp. 295-296).

Fig. 39. 9 rue Louis Boilly, where the psychiatrist Otto Rank lived and worked, only a few blocks from 47, boulevard Suchet, where Anaïs had lived earlier. Today Marmottan, the impressionist museum, is situated on this short street.

Fig. 40. 26, rue des Marronniers, where Anaïs stayed for a couple of months in a hotel with Henry Miller in 1933-34, while Hugh Guiler and Otto Rank thought she lived alone.

In January 1934, Hugh and Anaïs closed down their house in Louveciennes for the winter; it was impractical, with no central heating, and it seems that the Guilers' finances had improved so much that they didn't have to live there the whole year round. Hugh moved into a flat crammed with furniture at avenue Victor Hugo, while Anaïs remained at the hotel on rue des Marronniers, under the pretext that her psychoanalysis demanded it. Henry, who didn't feel at ease in the bourgeois environment, occasionally moved to a shabby hotel in Montmartre, but in February 1934 he was back at rue des Marronniers, where he and Anaïs worked intensely. Henry worked on his book about D. H. Lawrence (unpublished until just before Henry's death in 1980) and *Self Portrait*, later to be entitled *Black Spring*, a novel he had started to write at the beginning of 1933, while Anaïs continued to work on her second story about June, which she called "Alraune 2," and she had also started to write a new story, called in turn "The Double" and "Father Story." Later it was to be included in *The Winter of Artifice* under the title "Lilith."

In March 1934 Anaïs writes in her diary, which she had taken up again after a relatively short break, that "Djuna" was almost finished. On April 7, 1934 she sent the manuscript to Henry's literary agent William Bradley.

At this point Jack Kahane's publishing house Obelisk Press was close to bankruptcy, and Anaïs still hadn't succeeded in raising the money for the printing of *Tropic of Cancer*. It was because of this that Henry turned to Sylvia Beach, who had by now completed publication of James Joyce's *Ulysses*. She turned down *Tropic of Cancer*, obviously in a rather chilly way; Henry felt that she was a woman with "snow in her veins" (*A Literate Passion*, p. 231).

By the summer of 1934 Anaïs had made yet another psychoanalyst lose his head: she had started an affair with Otto Rank, who fell desperately in love with her. After some time Anaïs also fell in love, but she was still attached to Henry and met him as often as she could. On top of everything else, she also found she was several months pregnant although she had been told that she was sterile; she concluded that the father could only be Henry. Without hesitating, she decided on an abortion and sought out a midwife, who gave her quinine in order to provoke a miscarriage. But the summer passed and nothing happened.

In August 1934 Anaïs consulted a physician, who stated that she was in her sixth month; the abortion would now have to be carried out surgically. This painful event, which Anaïs describes in detail in her diary, was also the theme of the famous short story "Birth."

In September Henry sublet the studio at 18, Villa Seurat from Michael Fraenkel. Anaïs offered to pay his rent, something she hadn't told Rank, in order to avoid any complications caused by jealousy. Anaïs told Hugh that she had rented the flat at Villa Seurat on her own so that she would have a place where she could work undisturbed.

The condition set by Anaïs for renting the studio was that Fred Perlès was not to live there; Henry didn't oppose this as he preferred to live alone. At first Fred was deeply hurt and stayed away from Henry, but after some time the old buddies got in touch again and their friendship was to last for the rest of their lives.

Anaïs had first discovered Villa Seurat while posing as a model for the sculptor Chana Orloff, who had a studio in this idyllic little dead-end street in the 14th arrondissement, where several artists had ended up, among them Salvador Dalí. Henry already knew Villa Seurat and the building at no. 18: this was where Fraenkel had let him live for a period four years earlier, and it was here he had started to write *Tropic of Cancer*. The street looks basically the same today as it did then. The studio at no. 18 was on the first floor to the right and consisted of a big living room overlooking the back yard, a bedroom facing onto the street, a very small kitchen and a bathroom.

On the same day that Henry moved into the studio at Villa Seurat, *Tropic of Cancer* was published, including a brilliant and concise introduction by Anaïs Nin. Now Henry and Anaïs started to mail the novel to a number of established writers, such as Ezra Pound, George Orwell, Aldous Huxley and John Dos Passos, all of whom responded favorably.

For Anaïs this was the beginning of a disjointed period: in Louveciennes she was Mrs. Guiler, who didn't have to do a lot of housework since there was a maid; and at Villa Seurat she was Mrs. Miller, shopping, cleaning and cooking, even though Henry was in no way averse to housework.

Fig. 41. 18, Villa Seurat, where Anaïs rented a studio for Henry Miller on the first floor to the right.

Fig. 42. Villa Seurat is a small, idyllic dead-end street that hasn't changed much since the '30s.

At the same time Anaïs continued to be Otto Rank's passionate mistress and planned to join him in New York, where he was preparing to move for economic reasons. Rank had offered Anaïs a job as his assistant in New York, something that Hugh was not opposed to as he very much wanted her to break her bonds with Henry. But Anaïs and Henry had decided that Henry would come to New York, too, as soon as she had raised money for his ticket.

On October 7, 1934 Hugh and Anaïs went to a farewell party for the Ranks at 9, rue Louis Boilly. "A strange day," Anaïs writes in her diary. "Hugh and I went at four o'clock to Rank's apartment. There were people there, saying good-bye. I was dressed in a russet suit (the green suit dyed) and wore a veil and felt beautiful... Everybody said good-bye. They leaned out of the window while Rank drove away. Hugh and I stood on the curb, waving" (*Incest*, p. 393).

In mid-October Anaïs and Hugh had found subtenants for the house in Louveciennes during the winter and stored part of their furniture and belongings.

In the diary entry of October 25, 1934, Anaïs mentions that they have rented an apartment at 41, rue de Versailles, having decided to live half the year in Louveciennes and half the year in Paris. Thus Hugh would live in Paris while Anaïs was in the U.S. Rosa and Joaquín continued to live in 18 bis, avenue de Versailles.

In November 1934 Anaïs left for New York, where Otto Rank had rented a room for her at the Barbizon Plaza Hotel, 101 W. 58th St. She started work at once and became extremely busy as Rank's secretary. Soon she was also to start receiving her own patients.

In January 1935, Henry Miller arrived in New York, and he and Anaïs resumed their love affair. In May, Anaïs reunited with Hugh in Montreal, and when they came to New York, they stayed at 7 Park Avenue, apartment 61, where, according to a diary entry, the rent was 125 dollars. Henry moved into Anaïs's room at the Barbizon Plaza, paid for until the end of the month.

The love affair between Anaïs and Otto Rank had cooled drastically on both sides: Rank had discovered that Anaïs had lied to him about Henry and asked her to return his (Rank's) letters. Then he left for California on a lecturing tour. Anaïs was most likely relieved: Rank had started to dominate her life far too much. On top of her work as secretary and therapist he also wanted her to revise his books for greater clarity and linguistic elegance. "Work for a lifetime," Anaïs laconically states in her diary in November 1934.

In New York, Henry finished *Black Spring* before returning to Paris in May 1935, a couple weeks after Anaïs, who returned to Louveciennes with Hugh. She found her beloved house in a miserable state after the subletting.

"Louveciennes is old and tranquil," she writes in her diary. "I once loved its oldness, its character. It now seems to have the musty odor of the past. New York was *new*. The garden wall is crumbling from the weight of the ivy. My mother thinks it is beautiful. But I am sad. I do not seem to fit here any more, or am I in love with feverish activity, intensity, excitement? The silence of Louveciennes, the stony peasant faces behind the windows. Peace. Home is peace. The village bells are ringing. The smell of honeysuckle enters through the window. A new me does not belong here any longer, a new me is an adventurer and a nomad" (*Diary 2*, p. 42).

In the summer of 1935, Anaïs Nin, Henry Miller, Fred Perlès and Michael Fraenkel gathered in Louveciennes to discuss plans for a publishing house. Earlier Anaïs and Henry had dreamt of installing a printing machine above the garage in Louveciennes and begin printing their own books, but the project was never followed through. Now the four writers decided to start their own publishing house, at Fred's suggestion to be named Siana—Anaïs spelled backwards. Its address was to be 18, Villa Seurat. One of the first books they agreed on publishing was *The House of Incest*.

After the intensity of her life in New York, Anaïs found Louveciennes suffocating. She longed for life in a big city again. The apartment at rue de Versailles where Hugh had lived while she was in New York seems to have disappeared, for in October 1935, she and Hugh rented part of an apartment at 13, avenue de la Bourdonnais in the 7th arrondissement. Anaïs's French friend, the writer Louise de Vilmorin, had lived there earlier, but now she was divorced and her ex-husband, Henry Hunt, occupied a part of the big and elegantly decorated apartment with their children, and Louise had moved to her property in the countryside.

Now Anaïs began socializing with both Artaud and Allendy again and also participated in the bohemian life at Villa Seurat. The writer Rebecca West, whom Anaïs had visited earlier in London while trying to interest her in *Tropic of Cancer*, was present at one of the parties at Villa Seurat and later described how a drunk Henry Miller tried to have a bath fully dressed and would have drowned if she and Anaïs hadn't discovered him and pulled him out of the tub.

In January 1936 Anaïs returned to her patients in New York, once more accompanied by Henry. He seems to have worked as her assistant, occasionally receiving his own patients. Before going back to Paris in April 1936, Anaïs visited Otto Rank at his apartment on Riverside Drive, an encounter that was to be their last. Anaïs found Rank sad. He said he wanted to divorce his wife and start a new life in California. In 1939 he married his secretary, but in October of the same year he died suddenly as a result of kidney failure.

No sooner was Anaïs back in France that she and Hugh went on holiday to Morocco. On their return they found Paris afflicted by strikes and rumors of imminent war; Henry was depressed, and Anaïs felt weak and powerless. The only good thing was that *The House of Incest* was published, an edition of 249 signed and numbered copies.

By now Hugh and Anaïs had decided to leave the uncomfortable house in Louveciennes. It was difficult to find subtenants during the winter and it was too expensive to pay rent for a whole year while only spending summers there.

For Anaïs it was a heavy sacrifice to leave her beloved Louveciennes, and she couldn't write about the traumatic move until several months later, in October 1936. In order to "enter a new cycle" she had decided to sell most of the furniture and she organized an auction.

But, as she writes in her diary, she hadn't realized what an auction really meant; she was shocked to see it advertised with great hullabaloo in the village and appalled when curious locals flocked to the front yard, where the auctioneer had exposed "beds, curtains, carpets, tables, desks, chairs, bookcases, pillows, bedspreads, all the intimate furnishings of a house so much loved and lived in, so saturated with memories" (*Diary 2*, p. 138).

To the auctioneer's alarm Anaïs started to bid for her own furniture and bought back the big Arabic bed, her bookshelves and her writing table, all of which she stored in Louveciennes and later put into the first houseboat she was to rent.

AFTER LOUVECIENNES

(1936 – 1939)

In June 1936, Anaïs and Hugh moved into a big apartment at 30, quai de Passy in the 16th arrondissement (now 20, avenue du Président Kennedy). The Guilers would probably have liked to stay in Louise de Vilmorin's beautiful apartment in rue de la Bourdonnais, but there seems to have developed a schism between Anaïs and Louise when Louise recognized herself as Isolina in *The House of Incest*.

Now Anaïs had to decorate yet another place, without great enthusiasm.

"A new background created without hope or joy, without feeling of permanence or with a conviction of its rightness," she writes in her diary, referring to the bright and spacious apartment at quai de Passy (*Diary 2*, p. 84)

But once she had started to busily decorate the new apartment she began to like it. This time she was inspired by an altogether new style, already launched in the '20s by the influential Exposition des Arts Décoratifs held in Paris. The apartment at quai de Passy turned out to be "modern, simple, joyous, light. Orange walls, white wool rugs from Morocco, chairs of a natural pale oak and cream leather, a huge table of pine wood..."

Finally, Anaïs was very satisfied with the result and gave a big housewarming party with live music, inviting all her old and new friends.

Among the guests that evening was the peculiar astrologist Conrad Moricand, of whom Anaïs had heard a lot from a friend, and she had phoned asking the friend to invite him. Later she did a lot to help the extremely poor Moricand and remained his friend for the rest of her time in Paris. (In the mid-'50s, Moricand visited Henry Miller at Big Sur in California, an experience which Henry described in *A Devil in Paradise*.) Anaïs had also invited a certain Gonzalo Moré, with whom Henry had become acquainted at a reception. According to Anaïs, the two men had got on well together because of their common dislike of work and their predilection for wine.

Gonzalo came from a well-to-do family in Peru, where he had met the dancer Helba Huara, with whom he had fled to New York. There Helba was lucky enough to be employed by the Ziegfeld Follies, but after some time she became afflicted by deafness and had to leave working on stage. Helba and Gonzalo moved to Paris, where Helba performed at private parties with her own choreography, inspired by Peruvian folklore. Anaïs had seen one of her performances and was impressed by her artistic audacity. Helba was also present at the housewarming party at quai de Passy.

Soon Anaïs found herself embarking on an affair with the virile Gonzalo, attracted by his dark eyes, his flashing smile and his "wild black hair" (*Diary 2*, p. 85).

The destitute Morés lived in a humid basement flat at rue Boulard, nor far from rue Schoelcher, and Anaïs inevitably transferred her need to help others over to Gonzalo and Helba, now that Henry was becoming self-supporting. In the summer of 1936, *Black Spring* was published, dedicated to Anaïs Nin.

Fig. 43. 30, quai de Passy, where Anaïs and Hugh moved in 1936. Today the street has been renamed avenue du Président Kennedy and the house is no. 20, but if one looks closely one can still dimly see the old no. 30 behind the new one.

Previous page:
Fig. 44. Quai de Passy, a block farther to the right of no. 30; on the corner there is still a restaurant.

At 18, Villa Seurat, a young art student, Betty Ryan, had moved into the studio below Henry's. Both he and Anaïs were to become her friends. Shortly afterwards the famous artist Chaim Soutine moved into the studio opposite that of Betty Ryan. Soutine, a man of Lithuanian-Jewish origin, had been a close friend of Modigliani's. In his modest studio, Soutine kept his distance and was extremely mysterious. Nobody was really in touch with him until Henry invited him up one evening to discuss a problem: a disgusting smell of smoke was seeping out of Soutine's studio and Henry and Betty Ryan were keen to hear what he was up to. Soutine laconically informed them that he was burning a number of his canvases that he didn't wish to pass on to posterity. Henry managed to suppress his alarm and started a conversation with the gloomy and taciturn Soutine, who became less reserved when Henry asked him to tell about his childhood in a ghetto close to Minsk and about his early years in Paris, but after the visit Soutine withdrew again. (During the German occupation he stayed with friends in the countryside; in 1943 he died of an ulcer.)

From the flat at quai de Passy, Anaïs had a view of the Seine where she saw houseboats moored to the quays. She had long dreamt of renting a houseboat, and now she began looking for one. In the diary the story about the renting of a houseboat is so compressed that one gets the impression that there was only one boat, but she actually rented houseboats on two different occasions. In September 1936 she moved into the first, moored to the quai des Tuileries not far from Pont Royal, a bit below the Louvre and opposite Gare d'Orsay. The owner seems to have been Maurice Sachs, who advised her against renting it as it was very difficult to heat. In the expurgated version of the diary Anaïs refrained from renting it, and the farcical incidents with the one-legged, alcoholic captain, with whom she had to share the houseboat, were assigned to the second houseboat, *La Belle Aurore*.

Hugh found the idea of renting a houseboat completely crazy, bearing in mind the primitive and insanitary conditions of life on the Seine. He himself never set foot on either of the boats. But Anaïs's delight with the houseboat wiped out all her problems for the moment. Gonzalo christened the first boat *Nanankepichu*, which means "not at home" in quechua. *Nanankepichu* immediately became the refuge of their erotic passion.

Occasionally Henry also visited Anaïs on the boat and stayed the night. But their relationship, from the start an emotional roller coaster, was seemingly stuck in a down period. What's more, Anaïs didn't like the new novel Henry was working on, *Tropic of Capricorn*, in which she felt he reduced women to depersonalized sex objects.

Fig. 45. Quai des Tuileries, opposite Gare d'Orsay.

In a long letter in March 1937, Anaïs accuses Henry of being incapable of communication, criticizes his negative and reserved attitude, plus his numerous superficial acquaintances with whom she thought he was wasting his time. Henry admitted that Anaïs was partly right, but he also felt that there was something fishy going on. He had probably got a hint of Anaïs's affair with Gonzalo, and he encouraged her to put all her cards on the table, something Anaïs certainly never did.

Still, she thought highly of their friendship. "My connection with Henry is on a creative, an imaginative, a more impersonal level," she writes in her diary in the summer of 1937 (*Diary 2*, p. 206). Unlike Henry, Gonzalo's "talent is for the personal relationship. He is emotional, warm, loyal, devoted" (p. 206). Soon, however, Anaïs was to discover the more difficult aspects of Gonzalo's character: his total lack of discipline, his stormy emotions that too often swept reason away.

The complications of Anaïs's emotional and erotic attachment to Henry didn't keep her from visiting him at the studio on Villa Seurat, where in the spring of 1937 Henry arranged an exhibition for the German painter Hans Reichel, whom he had met the previous year. Reichel, an anti-Nazi who had arrived in Paris towards the end of the '20s, was plagued by economic problems. Henry arranged for him to exhibit his canvases in Betty Ryan's studio which had been freshly painted and was sparsely furnished. (Among the visitors to the unofficial exhibition was Hugh Guiler, who had no idea that Anaïs still spent time at Villa Seurat and

Previous page:
Fig. 46. From the apartment on quai de Passy, Anaïs had a view of the Seine and the bridge of Passy, which still looks very much the same.

that the people living there called her "Mrs. Miller.") Both Anaïs and Henry admired Reichel intensely. Henry wrote an essay about him, called "The Cosmological Eye," which was published in *transition* in 1938; later on this essay was included in *Max and the White Phagocytes*. Anaïs paid homage to Reichel in her short story "The Eye's Journey," included in *Under a Glass Bell*.

In October 1937, Henry's essay about Anaïs, "Un être étoilque," was published in *The Criterion*, the exclusive literary magazine published by T. S. Eliot in London. A year later he also got it published in an American literary magazine, *The Phoenix*. Whatever conflicts they had in their personal relationship, and however upset Anaïs was because of Henry's sexist attitudes in *Tropic of Capricorn*, Henry still fervently admired Anaïs and predicted that her diaries, once they were published, would be regarded as one of the great works of the century.

At the beginning of 1937 Hugh was transferred to the branch office in London of what was now called the City Bank and the Farmers' Trust, but Anaïs had no desire to join him there. She led an intense erotic and social life in Paris, which she had finally come to love and know intimately, and she had nothing in particular to do in London. Hugh rented a small flat in London and spent weekends with Anaïs in Paris.

In August 1937, Anaïs wrote a long letter to the American writer Djuna Barnes, who lived occasionally in Paris, thanking her for the novel *Nightwood*, which she deeply admired. In her letter Anaïs praised the "language, the knowingness, the beauty, the tragic quality, the transparent power of touching depths... The most beautiful thing I have read about woman, and women in love" (*Diary 2*, p. 239). It hurt her deeply that Djuna Barnes never answered her letter.

Miss Barnes had already visited Paris at the beginning of the '20s and had rented a flat in Montparnasse, where she frequented the literary circle of Sylvia Beach, who found her both charming and talented. Her first book, *A Book*, was published in Paris. Later, in 1928, she published *Ladies' Almanack*, under a pseudonym, an ironic work with camouflaged portraits of the women of the American colony in Paris. The book sold well at Shakespeare & Co. Wambly Bald dedicated an article to Djuna Barnes in the *Chicago Tribune* of September 2, 1931, when she revisited Paris. On that occasion she rented a flat far from Montparnasse, a district that she thought had long since ceased to be interesting as a meeting place or source of inspiration: "There is nothing left but a big crowd," was her laconic comment.

Rumors have it that Djuna Barnes was irritated by the fact that Anaïs had used the name Djuna in *The House of Incest*. Another reason for her avoiding Anaïs might have been her utter distaste for the works of Henry Miller.

Fig. 47. La Coupole, 102 Boulevard du Montparnasse, in the '30s, with its big, popular terrace. The café was inaugurated in October 1927, with a bar on the ground floor, two restaurant floors and a dance floor in the basement. Both La Rotonde and Le Dôme expanded and were modernized in the mid-'20s. Some of the patrons afterwards moved to Le Select, a more modest place that was open all night.

In September 1937, the owner sold the houseboat that Anaïs shared with the one-legged captain, and so she had to leave *Nanankepichu*, the same month Lawrence and Nancy Durrell arrived in Paris and stayed for some time at 18, Villa Seurat. Both Anaïs and Henry had for some time corresponded with the young Durrell, who had read and appreciated *Tropic of Cancer*. Anaïs liked the texts that Durrell sent her. On their arrival at the Gare de Lyon on a foggy autumn morning, the Durrells were met by Anaïs and Henry, who brought a copy of Otto Rank's *Art and Artist* with them as a welcome-to-Paris gift. The two couples immediately got on well. Anaïs, Henry and Larry frequented La Coupole together so often that they began calling themselves "The Three Musketeers of La Coupole."

The Durrells, who lived in Corfu, now commuted between the party life of Paris and their family life in England until May 1938, when they returned to Corfu. They were, however, to come back for a second period in Paris in December of the same year and they stayed on until May 1939.

Fred Perlès had managed to become editor of a magazine originally published by the American Country Club in Paris, *The Booster*, for which he and Henry were now writing surrealistic texts. Anaïs was appointed social editor, but this was only for the sake of appearance. She was, in fact, becoming fed up with the bohemian life of Villa Seurat. Furthermore, she had—although until then sternly opposed to any political involvement—started to attend antifascist meetings with Gonzalo and had heard La Pasionaria, Pablo Neruda and André Malraux. Not that she was convinced by their stereotypical, political language, nor by Gonzalo's Marxist comments, but compared to the commitment of these militant circles, the world of Henry and Fred must have appeared superficial and irresponsible to her.

In the spring of 1938 another opportunity rose to rent a houseboat moored to the quai des Tuileries. This time the owner was a French film actor, Michel Simon; his barge, *La Belle Aurore*, was equipped with a heating system and a bathroom, and Anaïs would not have to share it with anyone. She immediately wrote to Lawrence Durrell to tell him the good news:

"I've rented the houseboat! For 500 francs! Steam heating and bathroom and windows and everything I wanted—and it's floating—and it's wonderful! I'm so happy that I can't write."

Fig. 48. La Belle Aurore in quai des Tuileries, owned by Michel Simon, was the second houseboat Anaïs rented.

No sooner had Anaïs moved into the new houseboat than Hitler annexed Austria. Franco was encircling Barcelona. Soon Anaïs found herself opening *La Belle Aurore* for political meetings furthering the cause of the Spanish republicans. She also helped Gonzalo by printing leaflets and posters, assisted those Spaniards who were seeking refuge in Paris (the French were not allowed to receive them in their homes) and made great efforts to provide other Spanish refugees with visas to Cuba.

In September 1938 the threat of war became acute. Paris mobilized, women wept in the streets, and crowds queued up in front of the banks. Many people left Paris, among them Henry Miller, who panicked and fled to Bordeaux. From there he wrote to Anaïs, asking her to take care of his luggage: two suitcases were to be deposited at Kahane's and one at American Express. When she went to Villa Seurat to collect the luggage Anaïs was struck by the desolation of the house: without Henry, Villa Seurat had suddenly "lost its glow," Anaïs writes in her diary. "It began to break down. The rain and the wind came through a broken windowpane. The hot-water heater was worn out. The paint on the walls suddenly appeared soiled. The need of repairs appeared hopeless. Because life had withdrawn from it. Anguish about war dispersed us. Tragedy seeped into the houses, from outside. It could not be shut out any longer. Villa Seurat and other places once so illumined with life began to die under my eyes. Houses turn to corpses overnight when we cease to live and love in them" (*Diary 2*, p. 340).

But at the end of September 1938 the München agreement was signed, postponing the eruption of war by yet another year, and Henry returned to Villa Seurat.

In January 1939, Hugh and Anaïs left the big, expensive apartment at quai de Passy, almost at the same time as Rosa and Joaquín moved from Paris to New York. Hugh still worked in London, and Anaïs moved to a smaller flat, not far from the Closerie des Lilas, at 12, rue Cassini in the 14th arrondissement, closer to Henry and the friends in Villa Seurat. The flat consisted of a living room with an alcove, a kitchen and a bathroom. Anaïs told Henry that she lived next to the house where Balzac had written *Seraphita*, a novel Miller loved and upon which he had started to write an essay. (The essay was published the same year in the French magazine *Volontés*, as well as in the British magazine *The Modern Mystic*; it's also included in *The Wisdom of the Heart*.)

Installed in her new flat, Anaïs read the proofs of *The Winter of Artifice* that Jack Kahane was to publish in collaboration with Siana Editions. It was the Durrells who paid for the printing, and Nancy Durrell designed the cover. At the same time Anaïs stoically helped Henry read the proofs of *Tropic of Capricorn*, which was also to be published by Kahane's Obelisk Press.

The same month as Anaïs moved to rue Cassini, all houseboat owners were ordered by the river police to leave Paris. Anaïs had to rent a tug to pull *La Belle Aurore* down the Seine in search of a new mooring place, which she didn't find until far-away Neuilly, where she had actually been born.

"Neuilly! I have circumnavigated only to return to my birthplace. An omen?" Anaïs wonders in her diary (p. 303).

In Neuilly she sadly abandoned *La Belle Aurore* to its destiny; the houseboat was in bad shape, rain leaked in, and now it was too far from Paris to live in and maintain.

Fig. 49. 12, rue Cassini, where Anaïs lived during her last period in Paris. The house was built around the turn of the century, but still looks amazingly modern.

Fig. 50. The building at 7, rue du Général Henrion Bertier in Neuilly, where Anaïs was born in 1903, is still there.

In Paris, Anaïs's father had collapsed during his last concert; Maruca was firmly intent on a divorce, and Joaquin Nin Sr. was to move to Cuba. Before he left he visited Anaïs at 12, rue Cassini. It was to be their last meeting. In a letter that Anaïs received from her father after his arrival in Cuba, he tells her that he had fainted in the courtyard after leaving her flat.

Franco had emerged victorious in the Spanish civil war and, while more and more foreigners started to leave Paris at the prospect of war, crowds of Spanish refugees were arriving. Because of Gonzalo's political commitments, Anaïs was able to take a close look at the tremendous suffering caused by the Spanish civil war. In March 1939, she writes to Rosa in New York: "Paris is lamentably sad. The refugees are pouring in, with contagious diseases from bad conditions in the concentration camps... The French...they're letting them die like flies" (*ANAIS: An International Journal 3*, p. 79).

Two weeks after the publication of *Tropic of Capricorn*, Obelisk Press went bankrupt. Shortly afterwards Henry left the studio in Villa Seurat before the imminent war. He was to spend his last weeks in Paris at a small hotel before embarking on a trip to those French rural areas he was so curious about but had never had the chance to see before. Slowly he traveled towards Marseilles, from where he was to leave by ship for Corfu on July 14. Several months earlier he had accepted Lawrence and Nancy Durrell's invitation to come and stay with them. He had also started to long for Greece, having heard Betty Ryan's description of the Greek islands and their incomparable light. Henry was to leave Paris without nostalgia, looking forward to discovering a new country.

At the end of May 1939, Anaïs went to St. Tropez on the Riviera, where she spent her last summer in France. Hugh joined her for a week before returning to London. Then Gonzalo and Helba arrived, and her friend Jean Cateret, who slept on the beach. Her old friends Horace Guiccardi and his wife were staying in St. Maxime.

"I wish you could see me," Anaïs writes in one of her letters to Rosa, "you would never again worry about me. The days keep passing quickly—just being lazy. The longest and best vacation I ever had" (p. 86).

On July 12, 1939, Anaïs and Henry met in Marseilles and went to Aix-en-Provence, where they spent the last two days before Henry left for Athens. It was to be their last amorous meeting in France. Henry had been hoping all the time that Anaïs would come with him to Greece, but it seems she never had any such plans.

When Henry left, Anaïs returned to St. Tropez for another six weeks' holiday. It was to St. Tropez that Kahane sent the first copies of *The Winter of Artifice*, a novel that was unfortunately to be eclipsed by the war.

At the end of August, Anaïs went to London, where she stayed with Hugh until the end of September. When back in Paris without Hugh, she started to think of traveling alone to New York. Many of her friends had already left Paris, where a spooky pre-war atmosphere reigned. On September 2, a general mobilization was proclaimed. After eleven in the evening, there was a curfew. The shop owners covered their windows with green cellophane, and café windows were painted in blue. In their flats people glued paper strips onto the windows to prevent them from shattering in case Paris were shelled. Anaïs used paper strips in the colors of the French flag and made artistic patterns with animals and stars on her windows at rue Cassini. "Everybody stops to look and smile," she writes in a letter to Rosa.

In September, Jack Kahane died quite unexpectedly. His son was to be sent to the front, and the publishing house was closed down. Anaïs had bad luck with her editors: Edward Titus, who published her essay on D. H. Lawrence, had gone bankrupt, as had Michael Fraenkel who published *The House of Incest*, and now Obelisk Press had disappeared just as *The Winter of Artifice* was published.

"Everything we do now seems like a wake," Anaïs writes in her diary. "Dinner at Rosalie's, once so full of gaiety, now empty. Most of the foreign artists have been sent home by their embassies... [Paris] changed aspect, as if all the handsome and the young people have been drained away, leaving only cripples, beggars and old people behind, leaving only a grey city of men and women without magic... We were given gas masks. Lights in the buses like the pale night-lights in hospitals. You cannot count your change. I saw the outline of military gear against the moonlight. Farewells every night. Taxis driving slowly as in heavy fog" (*Diary 2*, p. 346).

Anaïs would have preferred to leave for the U.S. immediately, but the American embassy informed her that she couldn't leave until November. In a letter to Rosa she complains of the perpetual rain, the depressing atmosphere and the bomb sirens every other night. She spent her time closing down her life in France, storing books, paintings and household

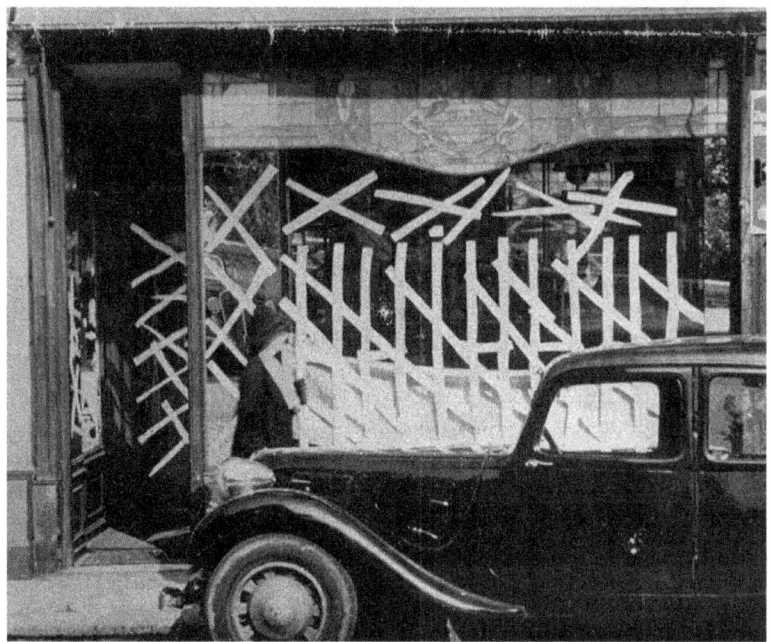

Fig. 51. In the autumn of 1939, the Parisians glued paper strips on their windows to prevent them from shattering if the city was to be shelled.

Fig. 52. Many, including Anaïs, seized the opportunity to make artistic decorations out of their taped windows.

utensils at a friend's place in Louveciennes; she deposited most of the diaries in a bank vault in Paris. Until the last moment she tried to get Helba to travel with her to New York; Gonzalo was first to go to Peru and later join them in the U.S., but it seems they didn't get their passports. (Finally they managed to leave France; in February 1940 both of them were in New York.)

In December 1939, Hugh arrived in Paris and Anaïs could finally leave with him. They traveled by train to Lisbon, where they took a hydroplane to Bermuda.

"We all knew that we were parting from a pattern of life we would never see again, from friends we might never see again. I knew it was the end of our romantic life," Anaïs writes in her diary (p. 349).

After World War II, many Americans returned from the U.S. to France: "I get attacks of homesickness, as each one leaves, and then I master it and try again to live here," Anaïs writes in a letter from New York to Henry in Big Sur in California in the autumn of 1946. "But last night I reread some old diaries and saw clearly how much bigger life was there. So again I hope to leave..." (*A Literate Passion*, p. 382).

In the summer of 1952, Anaïs expresses the same hope in a letter to Henry:

"I have a feeling we are all going back to Paris ultimately, where we were happiest. I don't think America has anything to love and I have grown to despise it. All of those who have gone back tell me they are no longer angry.... Well, here is to the day I will be walking down the boulevard and see you at a café table among your loyal friends" (pp. 390-391).

One year later Henry Miller went for a short visit to Paris but he was disappointed. The intellectual life, now dominated by the existentialist movement, appeared dull and sterile to him, and soon he was longing to be back in Big Sur.

Anaïs, on the contrary, found that life in Paris still had great charm and humanity on her first visit there after the war, in 1958, but her dream to return for good was never to be fulfilled.

REFERENCES

Bald, Wambly. *On the Left Bank*. Athens: Ohio University Press, 1987.

Fitch, Noel Riley: *Hemingway in Paris—Parisian Walks for the Literary Traveler*. Wellingborough: Equation, 1989.

----. *Sylvia Beach and the Lost Generation*. New York: Norton & Co., 1985.

----. *The Erotic Life of Anaïs Nin*. New York: Little, Brown & Co., 1993.

Jong, Erica. *The Devil at Large*. New York: Turtle Bay Books, 1993.

Klüver, Billy and Julie Martin. *Kiki's Paris—Art, Life and Love 1900-1930*. New York: Harry Abrams, 1994.

Laÿ, Jacques and Monique Laÿ. *Louveciennes: Mon Village*. Louveciennes: Jacques and Monique Laÿ, 1989.

Mathieu, Bertrand: *Betty Ryan, la Dame d'Andros*. Charlesville: Musée-Bibliothèque Artur Rimbaud, 1983.

Miller, Henry. *Black Spring*. New York: Grove Press, 1963.

----. *Max and the White Phagocytes*. Surrey: Calder Publications, 1970.

----. *Quiet Days in Clichy*. New York: Grove Press, 1987.

----. *Tropic of Cancer*. New York: Grove Press, 1961.

----. *Tropic of Capricorn*. New York: Grove Press, 1963.

Nin, Anaïs. *The Diary of Anaïs Nin, 1931-34*. New York: Harcourt Brace Jovanovich, 1966.

----. *The Diary of Anaïs Nin, 1934-39*. New York: Harcourt Brace Jovanovich, 1967.

----. *The Early Diary of Anaïs Nin 1923-27*. New York: Harcourt Brace Jovanovich, 1983.

----. *The Early Diary of Anaïs Nin 1927-31*. New York: Harcourt Brace Jovanovich, 1985.

----. *Henry and June*. New York: Harcourt Brace Jovanovich, 1986.

----. *Incest*. New York: Harcourt Brace Jovanovich, 1992.

----. "Living Through 1939—Letters to Rosa Culmell Nin." In *ANAIS: An International Journal*, no. 3 (1985).

---- and Henry Miller. *A Literate Passion*. New York: Harcourt Brace Jovanovich, 1987.

Perlès, Alfred: *Sentiments limitrophes*. Paris: Edition10/18, 1984.

AUTHOR'S NOTE

For the help during my work with this book I would like to thank the following persons: Pierre Auzépy, who answered all my questions about the house in Louveciennes, both by mail and during personal conversations, and who allowed me to use photographs from his family album; Betty Gordon-Ryan, artist, who wrote from her home in Greece to clarify details about life at 18, Villa Seurat, Paris; Jacques and Monique Laÿ, experts on the history of Louveciennes; Bertrand Mathieu, an American writer in Charlesville, France; Noel Riley Fitch, whose biography about Anaïs Nin was of great help to me; Gunther Stuhlmann, Anaïs Nin's literary agent in the U.S., who among other things helped me to find an unpublished photograph taken by Anaïs Nin in her apartment at boulevard Suchet; and my old friend Jean-Marie Le Huche, who provided me with the issue of *L'Illustration* from September 1939 in which I found the two last photographs, from Paris just before the Occupation.

ABOUT THE AUTHOR

Britt Arenander was born in 1941 in Stockholm, got her BA in 1967, then worked for many years as a journalist, later on as press officer at the Swedish Amnesty section; she was also international secretary of Swedish PEN for a couple of years. Since 1969 she has published a dozen books, mainly novels, and translated French and English literature, including six volumes of Anaïs Nin´s *Diary*. In 1982 she left Sweden and has since then lived in Italy, Denmark, France, Belgium, and the past 16 years in Spain. A digital version of *Anaïs Nin's Lost World* was published by Sky Blue Press in 2011.

PHOTO CREDITS

The Anaïs Nin Trust: cover; pp. 9, 11; Figs. 11, 17, 29, 48

Britt Arenander: Figs. 18, 19, 21, 34, 38, 42, 43, 49, 50

Pierre Auzépy: Figs. 15, 16, 20

Patrick Fabry: Figs. 8, 10, 26, 27, 30, 31, 35, 37, 39, 40, 41

L'Illustration, Sept. 1939: Figs. 51, 52

Kungliga Biblioteket, Stockholm: Fig. 2

Photothèque des Musées de Paris: Figs. 1, 7

INDEX

Allendy, René 62, 65, 67, 68, 70, 71, 77
"Alraune" (Nin) 68
"Alraune 2" (Nin) 71
Anita (Nin) 29
Art and Artist (Rank) 70, 89
Artaud, Antonin 70, 77
Auzépy, Pierre 33-34
Bald, Wambly 49, 52, 53, 54, 88
Balzac, Honoré de 13, 91
Barnes, Djuna 88
Beach, Sylvia 43, 45, 73, 88
"Birth" (Nin) 73
Black Spring (Miller) 73, 76, 80
Booster, The (periodical) 89
Boussinescq, Hélène (Boussie) 26
Bradley, William 67, 73
Brancusi, Constantin 17
Brassaï, Georges 18, 47, 49, 58
Buñuel, Luis 52
Canadian Forum, The (periodical) 43
Cateret, Jean 94
Céline, Louis-Ferdinand 58
Chicago Tribune (newspaper) 47, 49, 52, 53, 54, 56, 57, 65, 88
Cocteau, Jean 54
"Cosmological Eye, The" (Miller) 88
cummings, e. e. 45
Dalí, Salvador 76
Dardel, Thora 17
De Vilmorin, Louise 79, 82
"Djuna" (Nin) 71
Dos Passos, John 74

"Double, The" (Nin) 73
Du Berry, Madame 42
Du Brissac, Duke 42
Duchamp, Marcel 47
Durrell, Lawrence 89, 90, 91, 93-94
Durrell, Nancy 89, 90, 93-94
Emilia (maid) 32
Erskine, John 25, 26-27, 45-46
"Eye's Journey, The" (Nin) 88
"Father Story, The" (Nin) 73
Fitzgerald, F. Scott 22
Fraenkel, Michael 47, 73, 74, 94
Franco, Francisco 90, 93
Guiccardi, Horace 17, 23, 94
Guiler, Hugh 13, 17-19, 22-30, 32, 34, 36, 46, 53, 54, 56, 56, 59, 64-65, 67, 68, 70-73, 75-77, 80, 81, 84, 85, 91, 94, 96
Hansen, Mr. 22
Hiler, Hilaire 19
House of Incest, The (Nin) 72, 77, 80, 88, 94
Huara, Helba 80, 94, 96
Hunt, Henry 77
Huxley, Aldous 74
Joyce, James 43, 45, 46, 73
Kahane, Jack 67, 73, 91, 94
Kiki 19
La Belle Aurore (houseboat) 84, 90, 91, 93
La Nouvelle Revue (periodical) 54
La Pasionaria 90
Ladies' Almanack (Barnes) 88

Lady Chatterley's Lover (Lawrence) 43
L'Âge d'Or (film) 52
Lawrence, D. H. 29-30, 43-45, 46, 53, 56, 73, 94
Leboeuf, Emélie (Mme.) 33, 36, 38, 42
Leboeuf, M. 33, 36
Leboeuf, Mme. 36, 38, 42
Lebrun, Elisabeth Vigée 42
"Lilith" (Nin) 73
Louis XV 42
Louis XVI 42
Malraux, André 90
Max and the White Phagocytes (Miller) 68, 88
Miller, Henry 13, 18, 32, 42, 46-49, 52-54, 56-59, 62-65, 67-68, 70-77, 80, 84-85, 88-91, 93-94, 96
Miller, June 47, 53-54, 67-68, 73
Miralles, Paco 26, 29
Modern Mystic, The (periodical) 91
Modigliani, Amadeo 17, 84
Monet, Claude 42
Moré, Gonzalo 80, 84, 85, 90-91, 93, 94, 96
Moricand, Conrad 80
Nanankepichu (houseboat) 84, 89
Neruda, Pablo 90
New Review, The (periodical) 52
Nightwood (Barnes) 88
Nin, Joaquín 17, 70, 93
Nin, Maruca 17, 70, 93
Nin, Rosa Culmell 13, 19, 22, 23, 27, 32, 33, 56, 65, 76, 91, 93, 96

Nin, Thorvald 13, 22
Nin-Culmell, Joaquín 13, 18, 22, 23, 26, 27, 32, 33, 34, 56, 76, 91
Obelisk Press 67, 73, 91, 93, 94
Orloff, Chana 74
Orwell, George 74
Osborn, Richard 46, 52-53
Perlès, Alfred (Fred) 47, 54, 58, 62, 73, 77, 89
Phoenix, The (periodical) 88
Picasso, Pablo 54
Pissarro, Camille 42
Pound, Ezra 74
Praz, Valentine 70
Proust, Marcel 32
Putnam, Samuel 52
Rank, Otto 43, 67, 70-72, 73, 75-76, 77, 89
Reichel, Hans 85, 88
Renoir, Pierre-Auguste 42
Rodin, Auguste 17
Rubinstein, Helena 42
Ryan, Betty 84, 85, 94
Sacco, Nicola 47
Sachs, Maurice 84
Sánchez, Eduardo 32, 62, 65
Self Portrait (Miller) 73
Seraphita (Balzac) 91
Siana (press) 77, 91
Simon, Michel 90
Soutine, Chaim 84
Strindberg, August 16-17
This Quarter (periodical) 43, 52
Titus, Edward 42-46, 52, 94

Tropic of Cancer (Miller) 53, 54, 59, 65, 73, 74, 77, 89
Tropic of Capricorn (Miller) 85, 88, 91, 93
Ulysses (Joyce) 73
Under a Glass Bell (Nin) 88
Vanzetti, Bartolomeo 47
Varèse, Edgar 47
Volontés (periodical) 91
Voyage au bout de la nuit (Céline) 58
"Waste of Timelessness, A" (Nin) 44
West, Rebecca 77
"When D. H. Lawrence Found Himself" (Nin) 29
Winter of Artifice, The (Nin) 73, 91, 94
Wisdom of the Heart, The (Miller) 91
Woman No Man Could Hold, The (Nin) 47
Zadkine, Ossip 47, 69-70

Publications by and about Anaïs Nin from Sky Blue Press

Trapeze: The Unexpurgated Diary of Anaïs Nin, 1947-1955 (print, digital)

Mirages: The Unexpurgated Diary of Anaïs Nin, 1939-1947 (print, digital)

Auletris: Erotica (print, digital)

The Quotable Anaïs Nin (print, digital)

The Portable Anaïs Nin (print, digital)

A Café in Space: The Anaïs Nin Literary Journal Vols. 1-15 (print, digital)

The Winter of Artifice—Original 1939 Edition (print, digital)

D.H. Lawrence: An Unprofessional Study (digital)

House of Incest (digital)

Under a Glass Bell (digital)

Cities of the Interior (digital):
Ladders to Fire
Children of the Albatross
The Four-Chambered Heart
A Spy in the House of Love
Seduction of the Minotaur

Collages (digital)

The Novel of the Future (digital)

Anaïs Nin: The Last Days—A Memoir (Barbara Kraft; digital)

Anaïs Nin Character Dictionary and Index to Diary Excerpts (Benjamin Franklin V; print, digital)

Anaïs Nin's Lost World: Paris in Words and Pictures, 1934-1939 (Britt Arenander; print, digital)

www.ingramcontent.com/pod-product-compliance
Lightning Source LLC
LaVergne TN
LVHW051508070426
835507LV00022B/2991